Contents

NABI PUBLISHING, LLC
nabipublishing@gmail.com

CHAPTER 1

Hangeul 한글

Hangeul(한글) is the name of the Korean Alphabet.
Hangeul consists of 24 letters: 10 basic vowels and 14 basic consonants.
When you expand the Korean alphabet with fusion(**합용**:habyong), and laterally attaching(**병서**:byeongseo) there are extra letters; 5 double consonants, and 11 compound vowels.

• 10 Basic Vowels

ㅏ	ㅑ	ㅓ	ㅕ	ㅗ	ㅛ	ㅜ	ㅠ	ㅡ	ㅣ
아	야	어	여	오	요	우	유	으	이
[a]	[ya]	[eo]	[yeo]	[o]	[yo]	[u]	[yu]	[eu]	[i]

• 11 Compound Vowels

ㅐ	ㅒ	ㅔ	ㅖ	ㅘ	ㅙ	ㅚ	ㅝ	ㅞ	ㅟ	ㅢ
애	얘	에	예	와	왜	외	워	웨	위	의
[ae]	[yae]	[e]	[ye]	[wa]	[wae]	[oe]	[wo]	[we]	[wi]	[ui]

• 14 Basic Consonants

ㄱ	ㄴ	ㄷ	ㄹ	ㅁ	ㅂ	ㅅ
기역	니은	디귿	리을	미음	비읍	시옷
[gi-yeok]	[ni-eun]	[di-geut]	[ri-eul]	[mi-eum]	[bi-eup]	[si-ot]
g of good	n of noun	d of day	l of lime	m of mom	b of band	s of snail

ㅇ	ㅈ	ㅊ	ㅋ	ㅌ	ㅍ	ㅎ
이응	지읒	치읓	키읔	티읕	피읖	히읗
[i-eung]	[ji-eut]	[chi-eut]	[ki-euk]	[ti-eut]	[pi-eup]	[hi-eut]
silent/ no sound	j of Jay	ch of cherry	k of key	t of take	p of pan	h of hat

• 5 Double Consonants (Tense Consonants)

ㄲ	ㄸ	ㅃ	ㅆ	ㅉ
쌍기역	쌍디귿	쌍비읍	쌍시옷	쌍지읒
[ssang-giyeok]	[ssangdigeut]	[ssangbieup]	[ssangsiot]	[ssangjieut]
kk	tt	pp	ss	jj

• Syllabic Block (C = Consonant, V = Vowel)
Korean letters are combined to form syllabic blocks. A syllabic block is composed of a minimum of two letters, a consonant, and a vowel. Letters composed in a syllabic block make a singular sound. Written Korean letters appear as boxes, not as string lines. For example, when you write 'hangeul', the letters are grouped like '한글', not like 'ㅎㅏㄴㄱㅡㄹ'.

There are two types of syllabic blocks, C+V and C+V+C. The **first/initial consonant** (choseong 초성) is the starting letter of the blocks. And the **final consonant** (jongseong 종성) is the last consonant of the C+V+C blocks. The final consonants are often called **batchim** (받침). Batchim's literal meaning is support/pedestal. The **VOWEL** in the syllabic block is called the medial sound (jungseong 중성).

The first consonant and a vowel are mandatory parts of any syllabic block. For example, when you write 'baby' in Korean as 'agi', it should look like 아기, not ㅏ기.

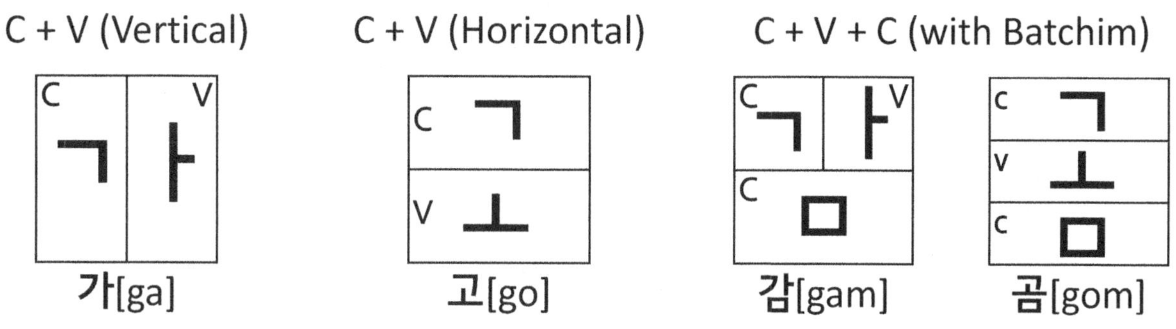

CHAPTER 2

BASIC VOWELS 기본 모음

The Korean alphabet, hangeul, was created in the 15th century by King Sejong of the Joseon Dynasty. At the time, the Korean alphabet was named Hunminjeong-eum (**훈민정음**). There are different versions of hunminjeong-eum books. One of them explains how it was created, and what principles that hangeul is based upon. According to the book, the vowels of hangeul are shaped after the sky(Heaven), the land(Earth), and humans.
The letter • (**아래아 / 하늘아** [a-re-a/ha-neul-a]; examples: ᄂᆞ ᄅᆞ) is no longer used as a stand-alone vowel in modern Korean.

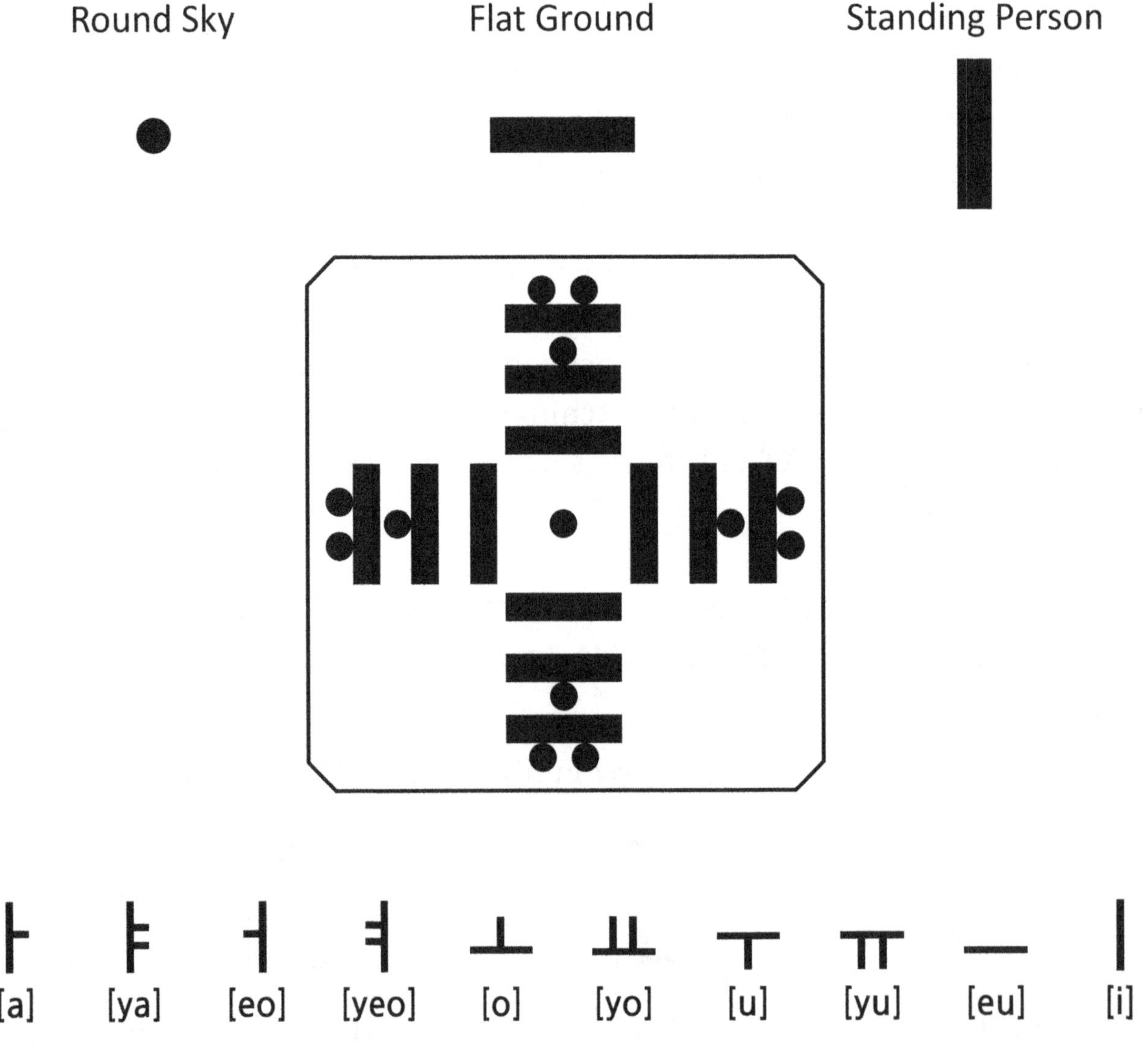

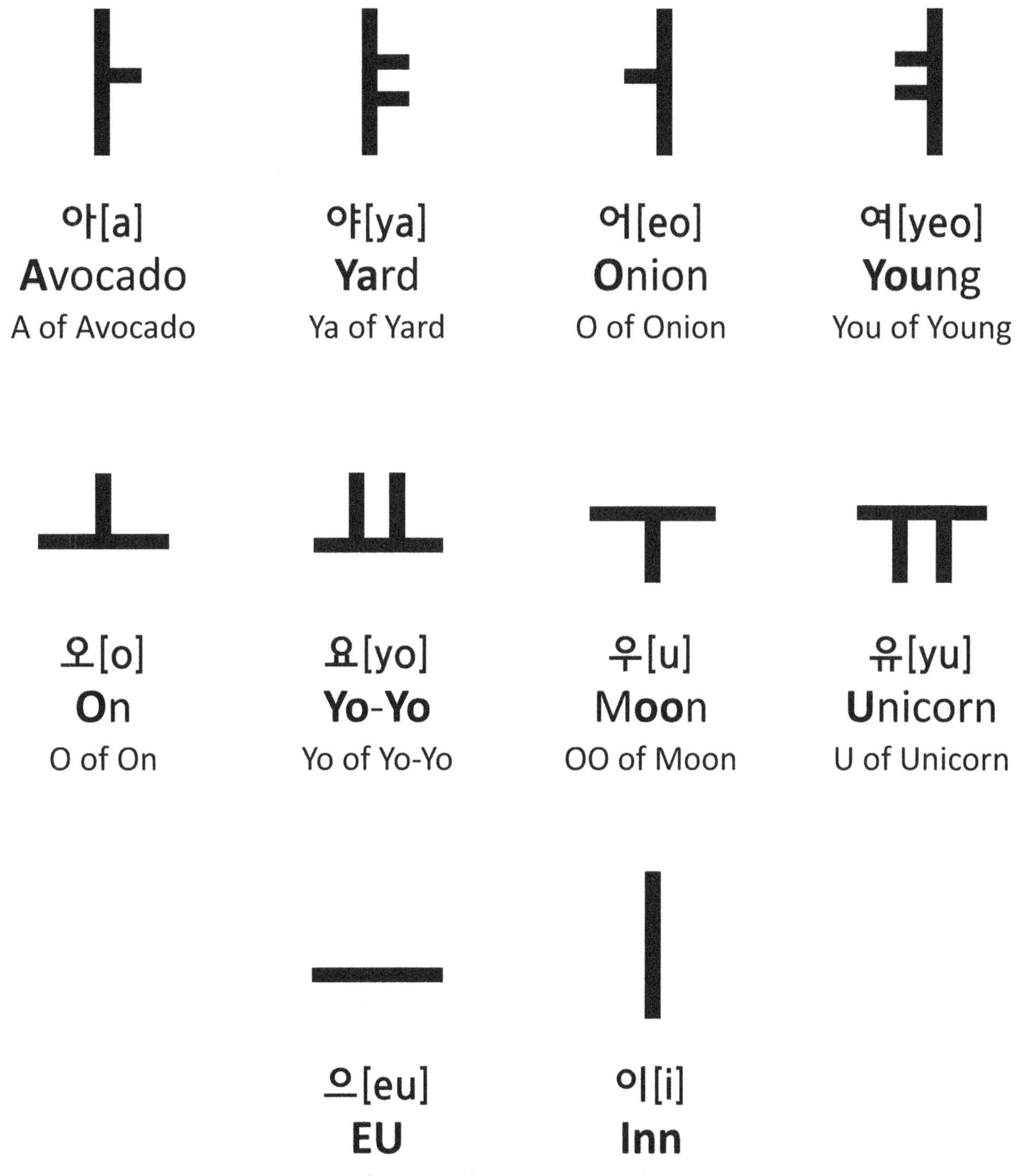
ㅏ
아[a]
Avocado
A of Avocado
ㅑ
야[ya]
Yard
Ya of Yard
ㅓ
어[eo]
Onion
O of Onion
ㅕ
여[yeo]
Young
You of Young
ㅗ
오[o]
On
O of On
ㅛ
요[yo]
Yo-Yo
Yo of Yo-Yo
ㅜ
우[u]
Moon
OO of Moon
ㅠ
유[yu]
Unicorn
U of Unicorn
ㅡ
으[eu]
EU
Green(gEUrin)
ㅣ
이[i]
Inn
I of Inn

CHAPTER 2

BASIC VOWELS 기본 모음
ㅏ 아 A, ㅑ 야 YA

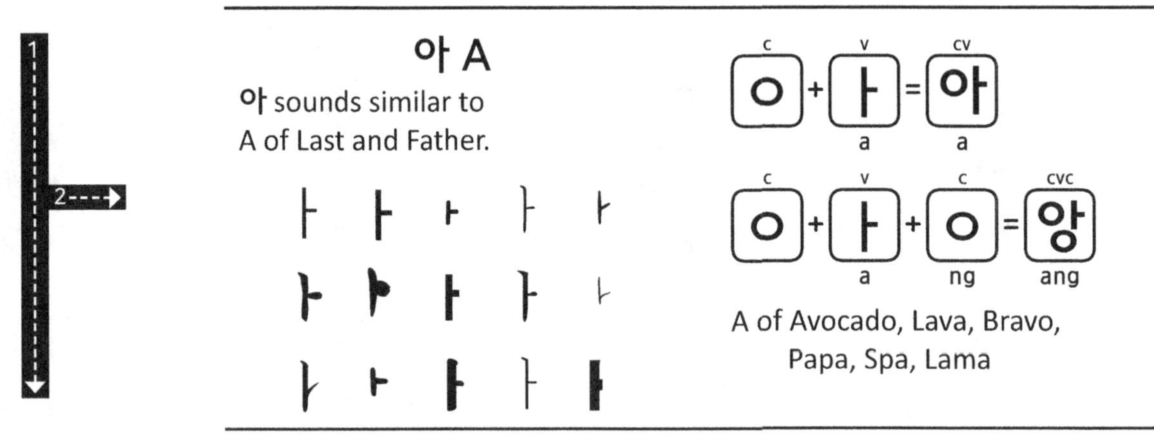

ㅏ	ㅏ	ㅏ	ㅏ	ㅏ	ㅏ	ㅏ	ㅏ	ㅏ	ㅏ
아	아	아	아	아	아	아	아	아	아

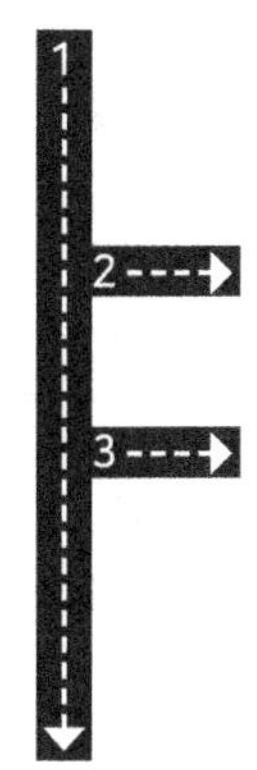

야 YA

야 sounds similar to YA of Yahoo.

ㅑ ㅑ ㅑ ㅑ ㅑ
ㅑ ㅑ ㅑ ㅑ ㅑ
ㅑ ㅑ ㅑ ㅑ ㅑ

ㅇ (c) + ㅑ (v, ya) = 야 (cv, ya)

ㅇ (c) + ㅑ (v, ya) + ㅇ (c, ng) = 양 (cvc, yang)

YA of Yard, Yarn

ㅑ	ㅑ	ㅑ	ㅑ	ㅑ	ㅑ	ㅑ	ㅑ	ㅑ	ㅑ
야	야	야	야	야	야	야	야	야	야

BASIC VOWELS 기본 모음
ㅓ 어 EO, ㅕ 여 YEO

어 EO

어 sounds similar to
EA of Early and OO of Blood

ㅓ ㅓ ㅓ ㅓ ㅓ
ㅓ ㅓ ㅓ ㅓ ㅓ
ㅓ ㅓ ㅓ ㅓ ㅓ

c v cv
ㅇ + ㅓ = 어
eo eo

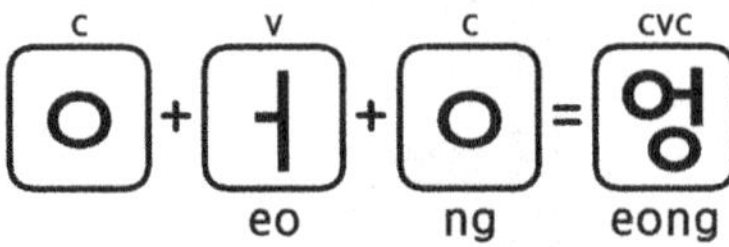

U of Bus, But, Gun, Up, Us, Luck
O of Onion, Honey, Money
OO of Blood, Flood

ㅓ	ㅓ	ㅓ	ㅓ	ㅓ	ㅓ	ㅓ	ㅓ	ㅓ	ㅓ
어	어	어	어	어	어	어	어	어	어

여 YEO

여 sounds similar to YOU of Young

ㅕ ㅕ ㅕ ㅕ ㅕ
ㅕ ㅕ ㅕ ㅕ ㅕ
ㅕ ㅕ ㅕ ㅕ ㅕ

c ㅇ + v ㅕ (yeo) = cv 여 (yeo)

c ㅇ + v ㅕ (yeo) + c ㅇ (ng) = cvc 영 (yeong)

YOU of Younger, Youngster

ㅕ	ㅕ	ㅕ	ㅕ	ㅕ	ㅕ	ㅕ	ㅕ	ㅕ	ㅕ
여	여	여	여	여	여	여	여	여	여

CHAPTER 2

BASIC VOWELS 기본 모음
ㅗ 오 O, ㅛ 요 YO

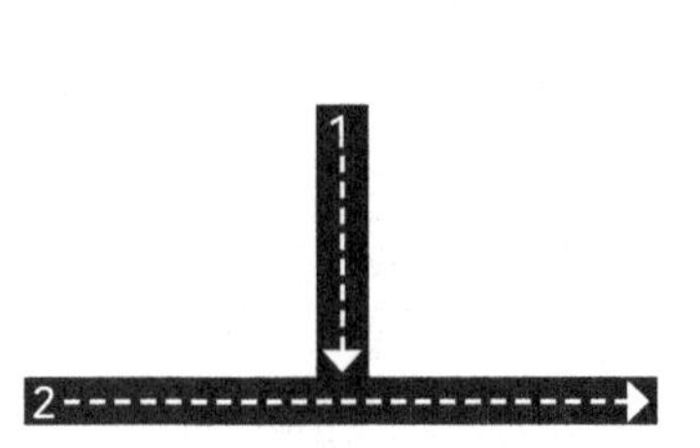

오 O

오 sounds similar to
O of Okay, Gold, and Ago

ㅗ ㅗ ㅗ ㅗ ㅗ
ㅗ ㅗ ㅗ ㅗ ㅗ
ㅗ ㅗ ㅗ ㅗ ㅗ

c ㅇ + v ㅗ = cv 오
(o) (o)

c ㅇ + v ㅗ + c ㅇ = cvc 옹
(o) (ng) (ong)

O of Ghost, Potato, Radio, Taco, Go, Most

ㅗ	ㅗ	ㅗ	ㅗ	ㅗ	ㅗ	ㅗ	ㅗ	ㅗ	ㅗ
오	오	오	오	오	오	오	오	오	오

요 YO

요 sounds similar to YO of Yoga and Yo-Yo

ㅛ ㅛ ㅛ ㅛ ㅛ
ㅛ ㅛ ㅛ ㅛ ㅛ
ㅛ ㅛ ㅛ ㅛ ㅛ

1 2 3

c ㅇ + v ㅛ (yo) = cv 요 (yo)

c ㅇ + v ㅛ (yo) + c ㅇ (ng) = cvc 용 (yong)

Yo of Yogurt, York, Yodler

ㅛ	ㅛ	ㅛ	ㅛ	ㅛ	ㅛ	ㅛ	ㅛ	ㅛ	ㅛ
요	요	요	요	요	요	요	요	요	요

CHAPTER 2

BASIC VOWELS 기본 모음
ㅜ 우 U, ㅠ 유 YU

우 sounds similar to
U of Flu, Guru, Rule, and Truth

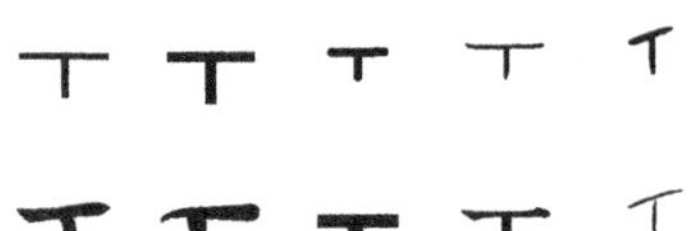

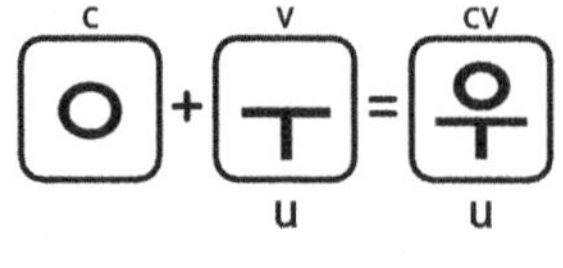

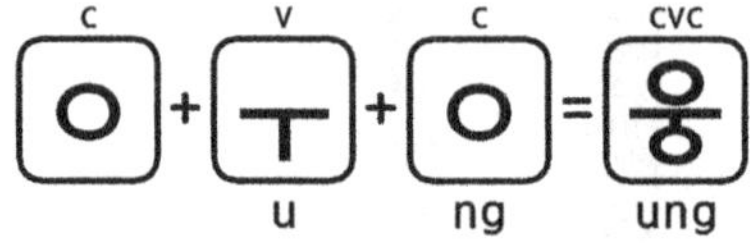

OO of Zoo, Moon, Food, Tool
UE of Blue, Glue, True, Sue
OU of Soup, Group

ㅜ	ㅜ	ㅜ	ㅜ	ㅜ	ㅜ	ㅜ	ㅜ	ㅜ	ㅜ
우	우	우	우	우	우	우	우	우	우

유 YU

유 sounds similar to
U of Uniform, and Unicorn

ㅠ ㅠ ㅠ ㅠ ㅠ
ㅠ ㅠ ㅠ ㅠ ㅠ
ㅠ ㅠ ㅠ ㅠ ㅠ

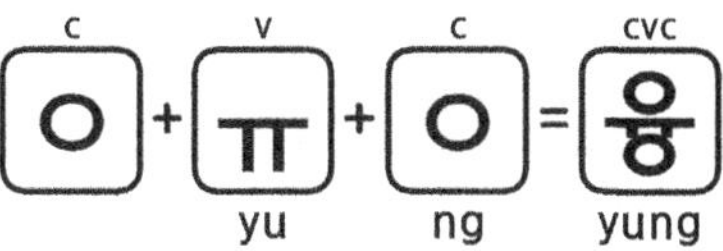

c ㅇ + v ㅠ (yu) = cv 유 (yu)

c ㅇ + v ㅠ (yu) + c ㅇ (ng) = cvc 융 (yung)

YOU of You, Youth
U of Utility, Usage, Unit, Use, Unique, Utopia

ㅠ	ㅠ	ㅠ	ㅠ	ㅠ	ㅠ	ㅠ	ㅠ	ㅠ	ㅠ
유	유	유	유	유	유	유	유	유	유

CHAPTER 2

BASIC VOWELS 기본 모음
ㅡ 으 EU, ㅣ 이 I

으 EU

으 sound is not used in English.
Alternative example:
Green - [그린/**geu**-rin]

ㅇ (c) + ㅡ (v, eu) = 으 (cv, eu)

ㅇ (c) + ㅡ (v, eu) + ㅇ (c, ng) = 응 (cvc, eung)

Slow - [슬로우/S**eu**l-lo-u]
Slide - [슬라이드/S**eu**l-la-i-d**eu**]
Spice - [스파이스/S**eu**-pa-i-s**eu**]

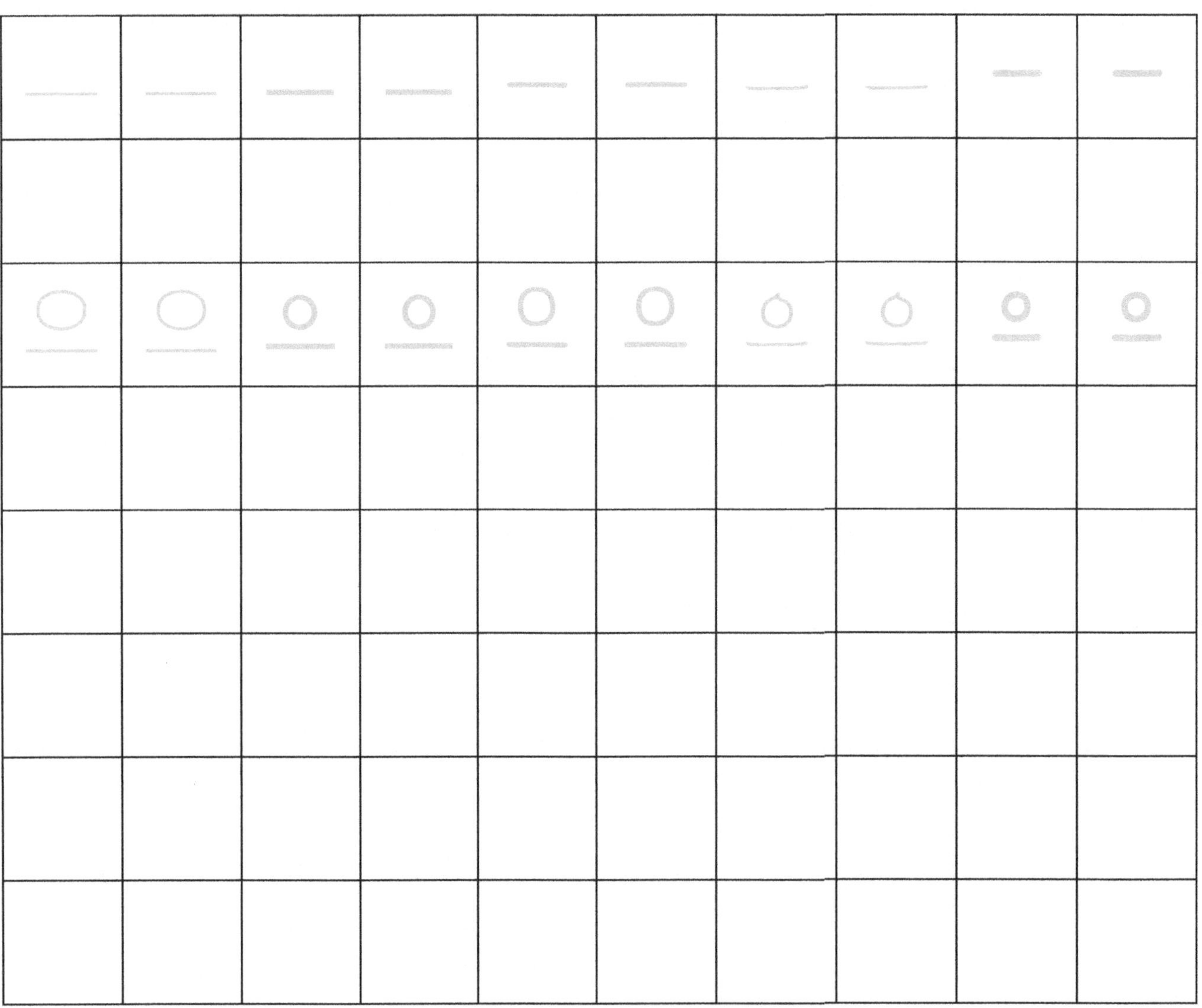

이 I

이 sounds similar to
I of Video, Big, Issue, and City

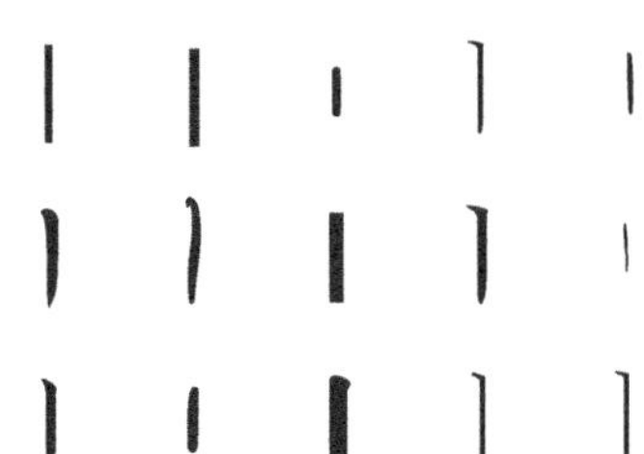

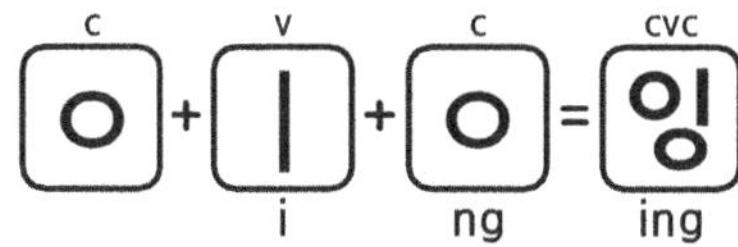

c v c cvc
ㅇ + ㅣ + ㅇ = 잉
i ng ing

I of Taxi, Is, Visit, Lip, Did, Music
Y of System, Crystal, Typical
E of Begin, Demand, Emotion

ㅣ	ㅣ	ㅣ	ㅣ	ㅣ	ㅣ	ㅣ	ㅣ	ㅣ	ㅣ
이	이	이	이	이	이	이	이	이	이

CHAPTER 2

Review 복습

1. Connect the Dots With the Matching Vowel's Sound and Example.

ㅓ •	• a •	• On
ㅛ •	• o •	• Avocado
ㅑ •	• u •	• **Ya**rd
ㅣ •	• eu •	• **You**
ㅜ •	• ya •	• **O**nion
ㅏ •	• yu •	• **You**ng
ㅠ •	• yeo •	• **I**nn
ㅕ •	• i •	• g**eu**rin
ㅗ •	• eo •	• **Yo-Yo**
ㅡ •	• yo •	• M**oo**n

2. Fill in the Blank Circles With the Basic Vowels in the Correct Order.

3. Write the Romanized Pronunciations of Each Word.

0) Yo-Yo 요요 [yo-yo]

1) Zero 영

2) Teeth/Two 이

3) Five 오

4) Cucumber 오이

5) Fox 여우

6) Milk 우유

7) Child 아이

4. Find Ten Basic Hangeul Vowels.

5. Write the Basic Vowels Under the Matching Pronunciation Five Times.

a	ya	eo	yeo	o	yo	u	yu	eu	i

CHAPTER

3 BASIC CONSONANTS 기본 자음

When hangeul was first created in the 15th century, there were 17 consonants (ㄱ, ㅋ, ㆁ, ㄷ, ㅌ, ㄴ, ㅂ, ㅍ, ㅁ, ㅈ. ㅊ, ㅅ, ㆆ, ㅎ, ㅇ, ㄹ, ㅿ). Three letters, ㆁ, ㆆ, and ㅿ, are no longer used in modern hangeul, and only 14 consonants remain (ㄱ, ㄴ, ㄷ, ㄹ, ㅁ, ㅂ, ㅅ, ㅇ, ㅈ,ㅊ, ㅋ, ㅌ, ㅍ, ㅎ).

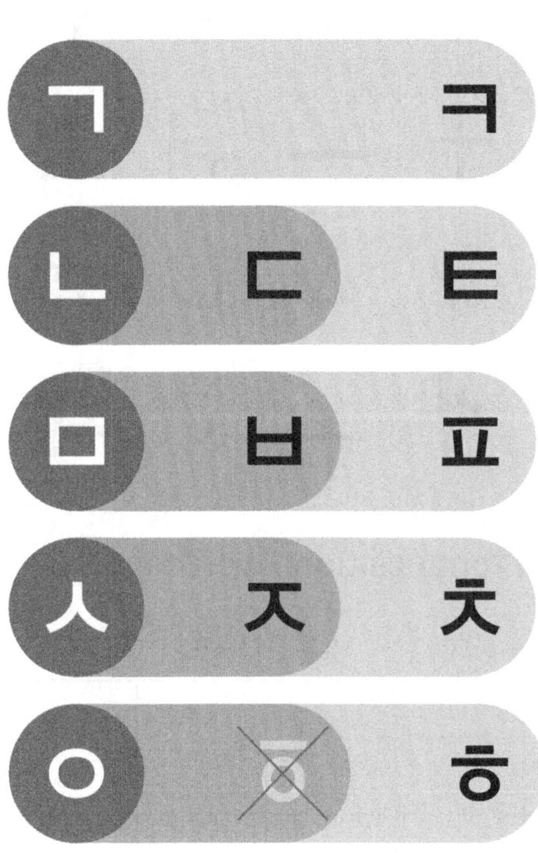

•Principle of **Adding a Line 가획의 원리**
Most consonants were created by adding a line to the five base letters (ㄱ,ㄴ,ㅁ,ㅅ,ㅇ). ㄱ-ㅋ, ㄴ-ㄷ-ㅌ, ㅁ-ㅂ-ㅍ, ㅅ-ㅈ-ㅊ, ㅇ-ㅎ. The three letters ㆁ, ㄹ and ㅿ were exempt from this principle.

• Most consonants have different sounds depending on the position inside the syllabic block. The name of each consonant has information about the pronunciation when used as the first and final consonant. For example, when ㄱ ***g***i-yeo***k*** is the first consonant, it sounds similar to ***g***. But, as the final consonant, it sounds similar to ***k***.

• **Basic Linking** (When the silent consonant ㅇ i-eung is the first consonant)
Linking is not a new concept for English speakers. It frequently occurs in everyday speech. For example, 'Did you - dijou' and 'how is it going - howzit going'. Basic linking with the letter ㅇ (ieung) occurs when ieung is the first consonant, and there is a final consonant in front of i-eung's syllabic block.

문어 -> [무너]	물어 -> [무러]
mun-eo -> muneo	mul-eo -> mureo

ㄱ
기역[gi-yeok]
G of Gorilla
Final C: k of cook

ㄴ
니은[ni-eun]
N of Noon
Final C: n of noon

ㄷ
디귿[di-geut]
D of Door
Final C: t of at

리을[ri-eul]
R of Rabbit
Final C: l of angel

미음[mi-eum]
M of Mom
Final C: m of mom

ㅂ
비읍[bi-eup]
B of Band
Final C: p of app

ㅅ
시옷[si-ot]
S of Snail
Final C: t of at

ㅇ
이응[i-eung]
Silent
Final C: ng of song

ㅈ
지읒 [ji-eut]
J of Jungle
Final C: t of at

ㅊ
치읓 [chi-eut]
Ch of Cherry
Final C: t of at

ㅋ
키읔 [ki-euk]
K of Key
Final C: k of cook

ㅌ
티읕 [ti-eut]
T of Take
Final C: t of at

ㅍ
피읖[pi-eup]
P of Pan
Final C: p of app

ㅎ
히읗[hi-eut]
H of Hat
Final C: t of at

CHAPTER 3

BASIC CONSONANTS 기본 자음
ㄱ 기역 GIYEOK

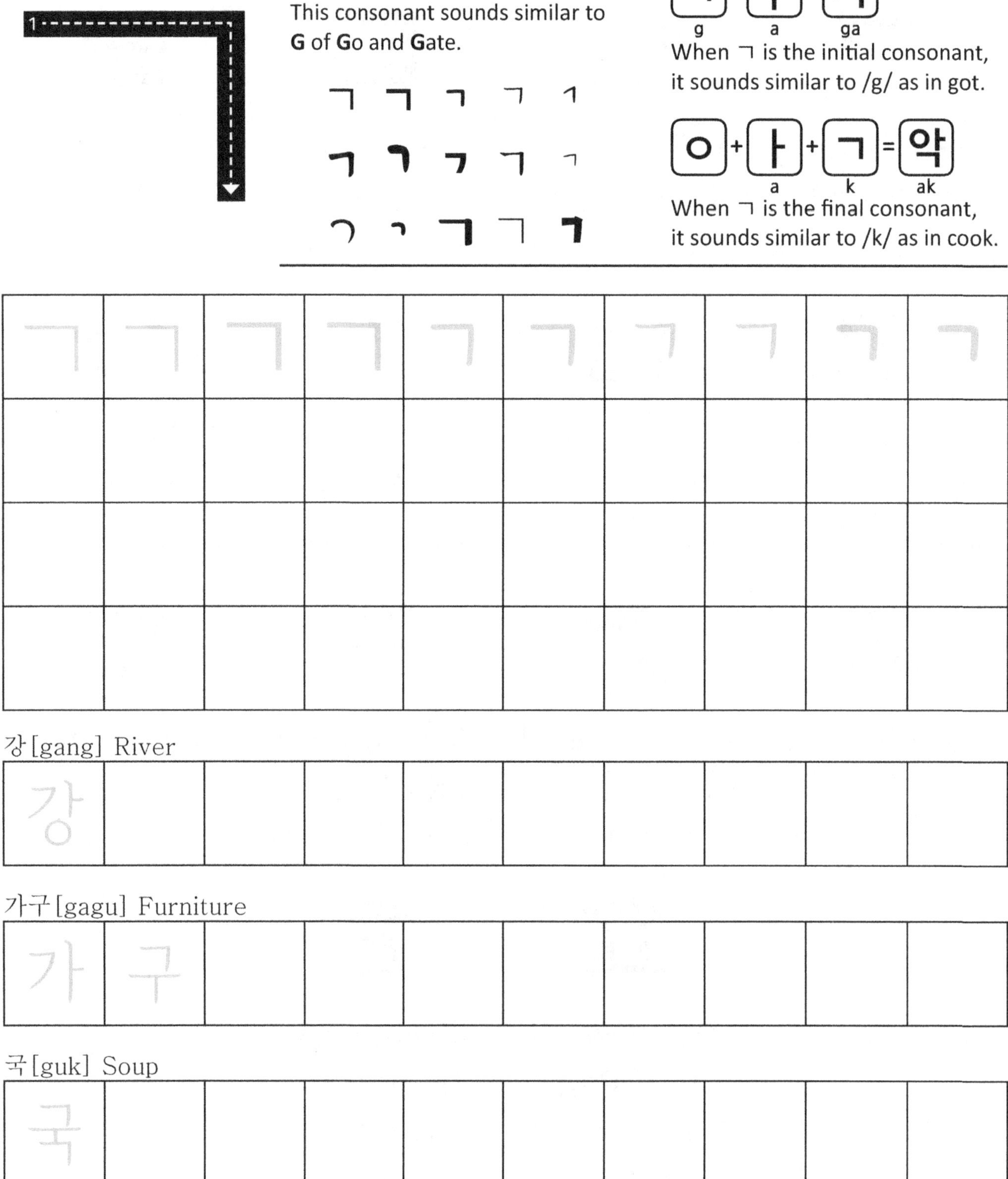

기역 GI-YEOK [g/k]

This consonant sounds similar to **G** of **G**o and **G**ate.

ㄱ + ㅏ = 가
g a ga

When ㄱ is the initial consonant, it sounds similar to /g/ as in got.

ㅇ + ㅏ + ㄱ = 악
a k ak

When ㄱ is the final consonant, it sounds similar to /k/ as in cook.

강[gang] River

가구[gagu] Furniture

국[guk] Soup

[ga]	[gya]	[geo]	[gyeo]	[go]	[gyo]	[gu]	[gyu]	[geu]	[gi]
가	갸	거	겨	고	교	구	규	그	기
가	갸	거	겨	고	교	구	규	그	기
가	갸	거	겨	고	교	구	규	그	기
가	갸	거	겨	고	교	구	규	그	기
가	갸	거	겨	고	교	구	규	그	기
악	약	억	역	옥	욕	욱	육	윽	익
[ak]	[yak]	[eok]	[yeok]	[ok]	[yok]	[uk]	[yuk]	[euk]	[ik]

CHAPTER 3

BASIC CONSONANTS 기본 자음
ㄴ 니은 NIEUN

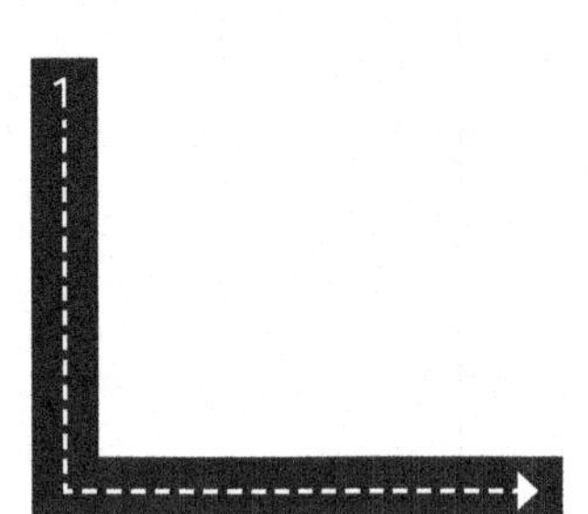

니은 NI-EUN [n]

This consonant sounds similar to **N** of **N**ow, **N**ame and **N**oun.

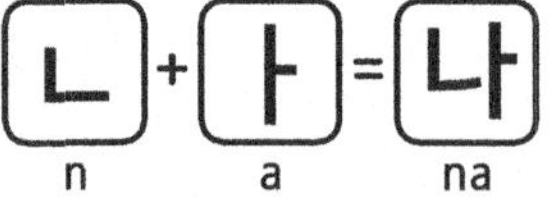

ㄴ sounds like /n/ in both positions as the initial or final consonant.

눈[nun] Snow/Eye (동음이의어 Homonym)

가난[ga−nan] Poverty

기능[gi−neung] Function

나	냐	너	녀	노	뇨	누	뉴	느	니
나	냐	너	녀	노	뇨	누	뉴	느	니
나	냐	너	녀	노	뇨	누	뉴	느	니
나	냐	너	녀	노	뇨	누	뉴	느	니
나	냐	너	녀	노	뇨	누	뉴	느	니
안	얀	언	연	온	욘	운	윤	은	인

BASIC CONSONANTS 기본 자음
ㄷ 디귿 DIGEUT

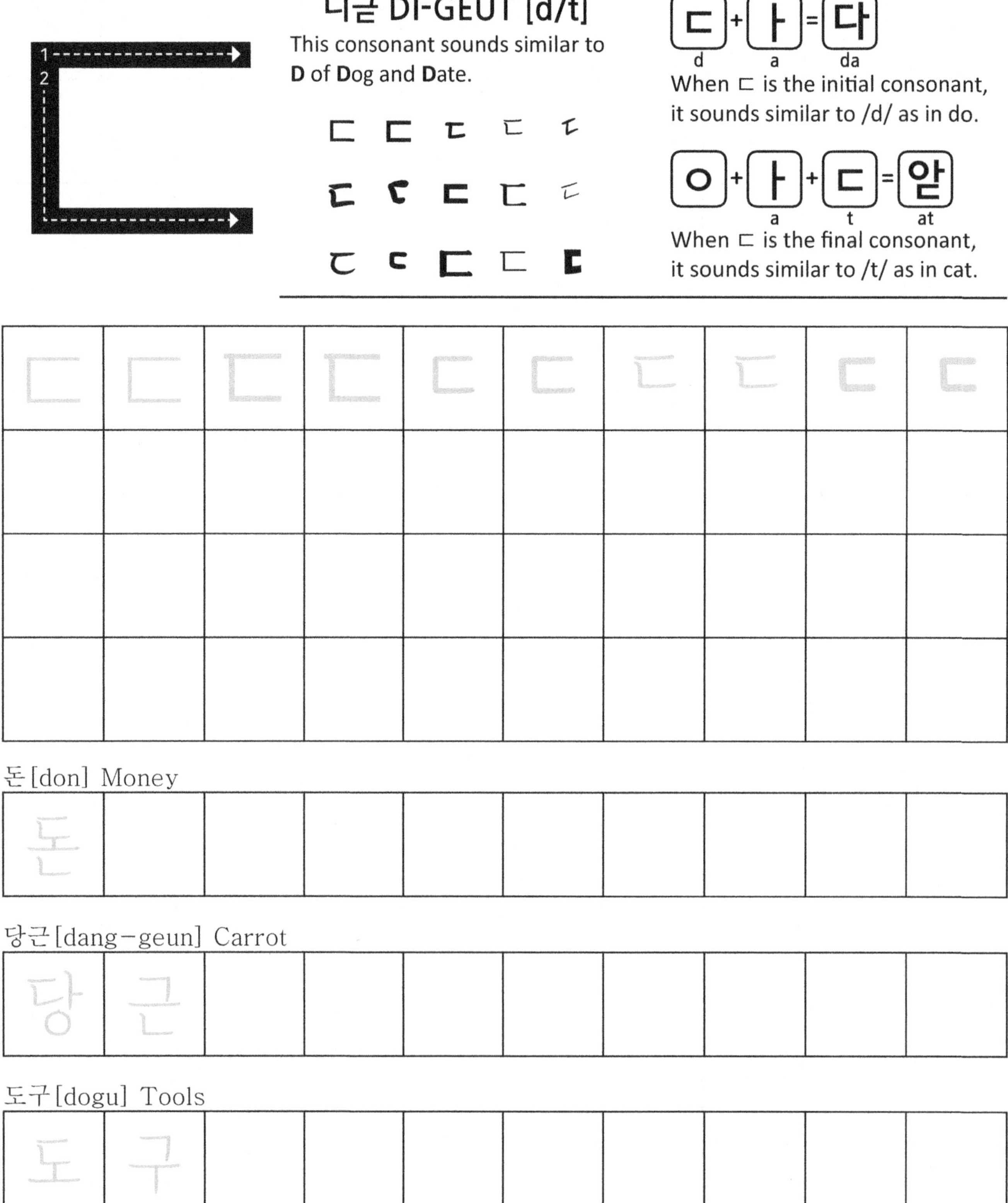

다	댜	더	뎌	도	됴	두	듀	드	디
다	댜	더	뎌	도	됴	두	듀	드	디
다	댜	더	뎌	도	됴	두	듀	드	디
다	댜	더	뎌	도	됴	두	듀	드	디
다	댜	더	뎌	도	됴	두	듀	드	디
안	얀	언	연	온	욘	운	윤	은	인

CHAPTER 3

BASIC CONSONANTS 기본 자음
ㄹ 리을 RIEUL

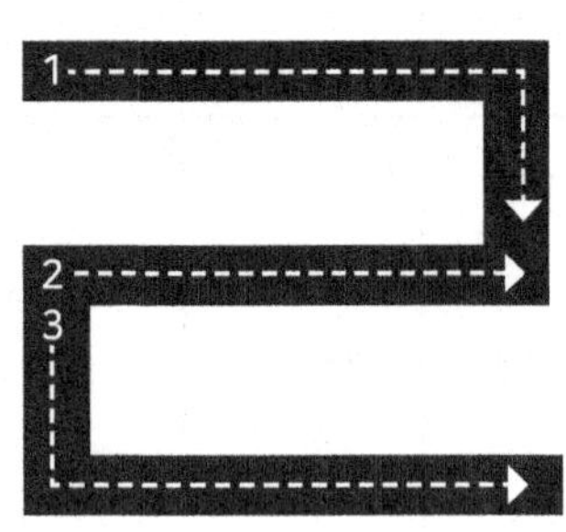

리을 RI-EUL [r/l]

This consonant sounds similar to **R/L** of **R**amen, **L**emon and **Roll**.

ㄹ ㄹ ㄹ ㄹ ㄹ
ㄹ ㄹ ㄹ ㄹ ㄹ
ㄹ ㄹ ㄹ ㄹ ㄹ

ㄹ + ㅏ = 라
L A LA

When ㄹ is the initial consonant, it sounds similar to /r/ as in row.

When ㄹ is the final consonant, it sounds similar to /l/ as in all.

ㄹ	ㄹ	ㄹ	ㄹ	ㄹ	ㄹ	ㄹ	ㄹ	ㄹ	ㄹ

달 [dal] Moon

달									

노랑 [no-rang] Yellow

노	랑								

기린 [girin] Giraffe

기	린								

라	랴	러	려	로	료	루	류	르	리
라	랴	러	려	로	료	루	류	르	리
라	랴	러	려	로	료	루	류	르	리
라	랴	러	려	로	료	루	류	르	리
라	랴	러	려	로	료	루	류	르	리
알	얄	얼	열	올	욜	울	율	을	일

CHAPTER 3

BASIC CONSONANTS 기본 자음
ㅁ 미음 MIEUM

미음 MI-EUM [m]

This consonant sounds similar to **M** of **M**oon, **M**o**m** and **M**aze.

ㅁ + ㅏ = 마
m a ma

ㅇ + ㅏ + ㅁ = 암
a m am

ㅁ sounds like /m/ in both positions as the initial or final consonant.

몸[mom] Body

몸									

물[mul] Water

물									

레몬[remon] Lemon

레	몬								

마	먀	머	며	모	묘	무	뮤	므	미
마	먀	머	며	모	묘	무	뮤	므	미
마	먀	머	며	모	묘	무	뮤	므	미
마	먀	머	며	모	묘	무	뮤	므	미
마	먀	머	며	모	묘	무	뮤	므	미
맘	먐	멈	몀	몸	묨	뭄	뮴	믐	밈

CHAPTER 3

BASIC CONSONANTS 기본 자음
ㅂ 비읍 BIEUP

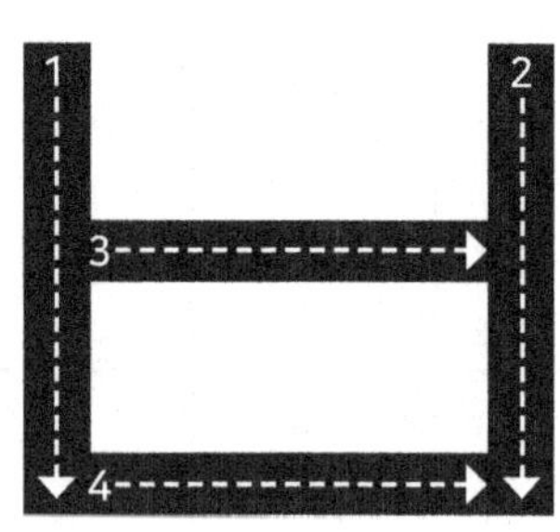

비읍 BI-EUP [b/p]

This consonant sounds similar to **B** of **B**ear and **B**eetle.

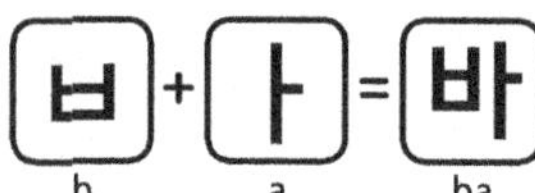

When ㅂ is the initial consonant, it sounds similar to /b/ as in be.

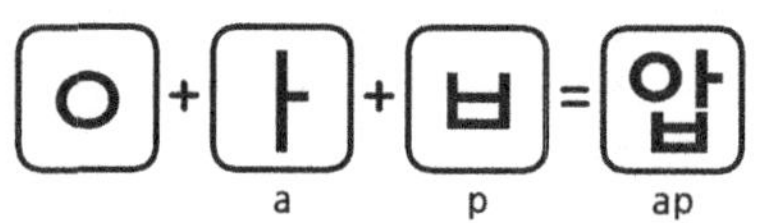

When ㅂ is the final consonant, it sounds similar to /p/ as in app.

ㅂ	ㅂ	ㅂ	ㅂ	ㅂ	ㅂ	ㅂ	ㅂ	ㅂ	ㅂ

봄 [bom] Spring

봄									

삽 [sap] Shovel

삽									

바람 [ba–ram] Wind

바	람								

바	뱌	버	벼	보	뵤	부	뷰	브	비
바	뱌	버	벼	보	뵤	부	뷰	브	비
바	뱌	버	벼	보	뵤	부	뷰	브	비
바	뱌	버	벼	보	뵤	부	뷰	브	비
바	뱌	버	벼	보	뵤	부	뷰	브	비
압	얍	업	엽	옵	욥	웁	윱	읍	입

CHAPTER 3

BASIC CONSONANTS 기본 자음
ㅅ 시옷 SIOT

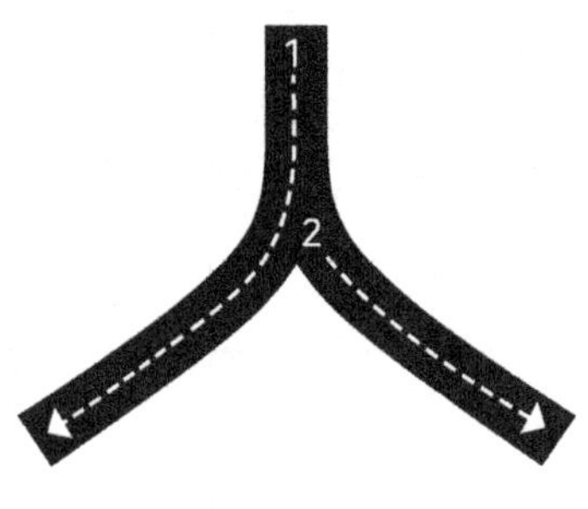

시옷 SI-OT [s/t]

Siot sounds similar to **S** of **S**now and **S**low. But when it is followed by ㅑ, ㅒ, ㅕ, ㅖ, ㅛ, ㅟ or ㅠ, it sounds similar to **Sh** of **Sh**ine and **sh**e.

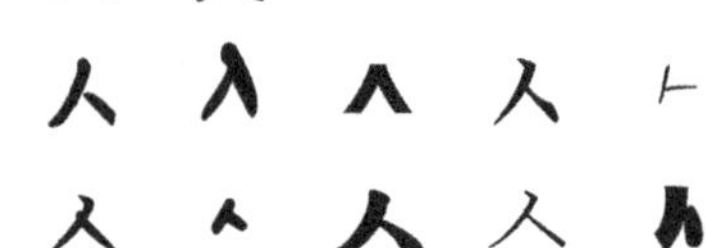

ㅅ + ㅏ = 사
s a sa

When ㅅ is the initial consonant, it sounds similar to /s/ as in sky.

ㅇ + ㅏ + ㅅ = 앗
a t at

When ㅅ is the final consonant, it sounds similar to /t/ as in cat.

ㅅ	ㅅ	ㅅ	ㅅ	ㅅ	ㅅ	ㅅ	ㅅ	ㅅ	ㅅ

소[so] Cow

소									

옷[ot] Clothes

옷									

소리[sori] Sound

소	리								

사	샤	서	셔	소	쇼	수	슈	스	시
사	샤	서	셔	소	쇼	수	슈	스	시
사	샤	서	셔	소	쇼	수	슈	스	시
사	샤	서	셔	소	쇼	수	슈	스	시
사	샤	서	셔	소	쇼	수	슈	스	시
앗	얏	엇	엿	옷	욧	웃	윳	읏	잇

CHAPTER 3

BASIC CONSONANTS 기본 자음
ㅇ 이응 IEUNG

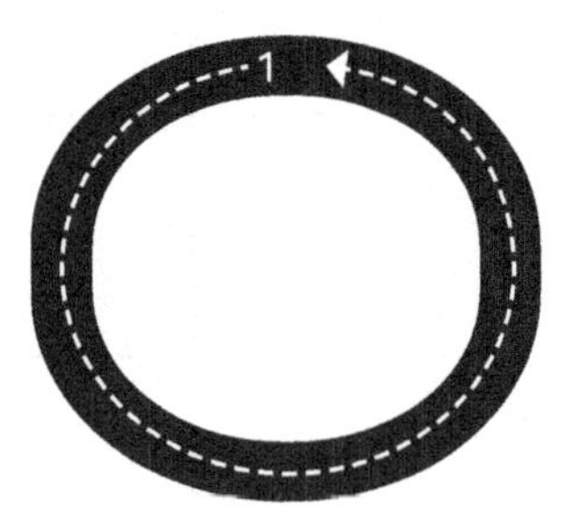

ㅇ 이응 I-EUNG [-/ng]

Ieung is a silent consonant.
As final consonant, it sounds similar to **NG** of Ri**ng** and Lo**ng**.

ㅇ ㅇ ㅇ ㅇ ㅇ

ㅇ ㅇ ㅇ ㅇ ㅇ

ㅇ ㅇ ㅇ ㅇ ㅇ

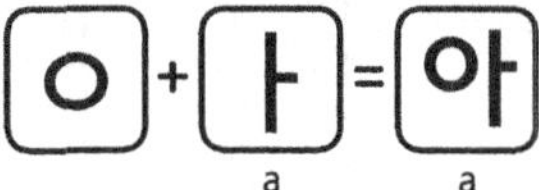

When ㅇ is the initial consonant, it has no sound.

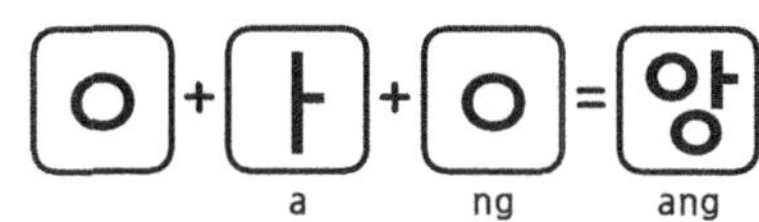

When ㅇ is the final consonant, it sounds similar to /ng/ as in sing.

ㅇ	ㅇ	ㅇ	ㅇ	ㅇ	ㅇ	ㅇ	ㅇ	ㅇ	ㅇ

상 [sang] Prize

상									

오늘 [o-neul] Today

오	늘								

이야기 [i-ya-gi] Story

이	야	기							

아	야	어	여	오	요	우	유	으	이
아	야	어	여	오	요	우	유	으	이
아	야	어	여	오	요	우	유	으	이
아	야	어	여	오	요	우	유	으	이
아	야	어	여	오	요	우	유	으	이
앙	양	엉	영	옹	용	웅	융	응	잉

CHAPTER 3

BASIC CONSONANTS 기본 자음
ㅈ 지읒 JIEUT

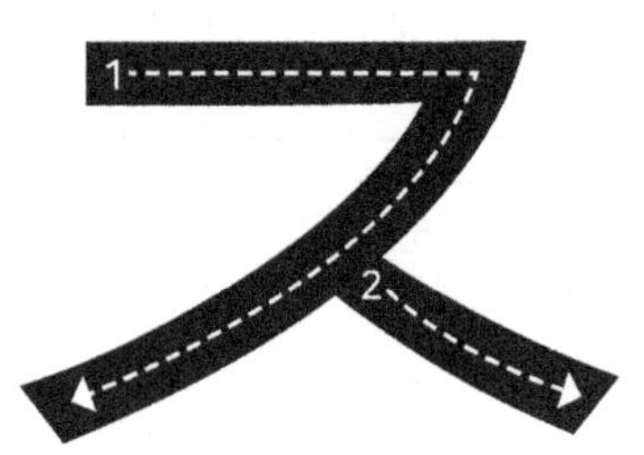

지읒 JI-EUT [j/t]

This consonant sounds similar to J of Jelly and Joy.

ㅈ ㅈ ㅈ ㅈ ㅈ
ㅈ ㅈ ㅈ ㅈ ㅈ
ㅈ ㅈ ㅈ ㅈ ㅈ

ㅈ + ㅏ = 자
j a ja

When ㅈ is the initial consonant, it sounds similar to /j/ as in joke.

ㅇ + ㅏ + ㅈ = 앚
a t at

When ㅈ is the final consonant, it sounds similar to /t/ as in at.

ㅈ	ㅈ	ㅈ	ㅈ	ㅈ	ㅈ	ㅈ	ㅈ	ㅈ	ㅈ

자[ja] Ruler

자									

잠[jam] Sleep

잠									

낮[nat] Daytime

낮									

자	쟈	저	져	조	죠	주	쥬	즈	지
자	쟈	저	져	조	죠	주	쥬	즈	지
자	쟈	저	져	조	죠	주	쥬	즈	지
자	쟈	저	져	조	죠	주	쥬	즈	지
자	쟈	저	져	조	죠	주	쥬	즈	지
앗	얏	엇	엿	옷	욧	웃	윳	읏	잇

CHAPTER 3

BASIC CONSONANTS 기본 자음
ㅊ 치읓 CHIEUT

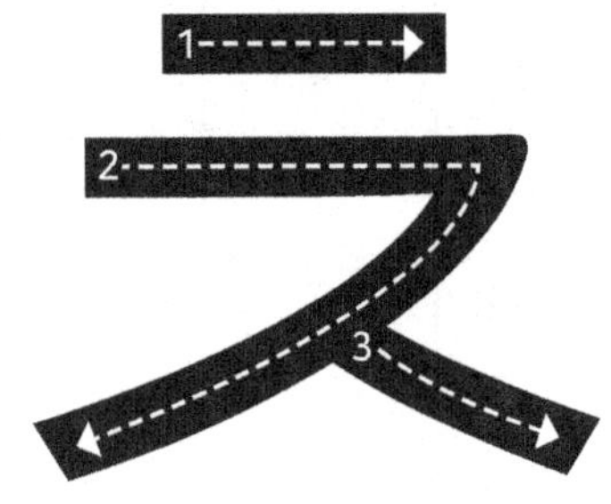

치읓 CHI-EUT [ch/t]

This consonant sounds similar to **CH** of **CH**ess and **CH**eese.

ㅊ + ㅏ = 차
ch a cha

When ㅊ is the initial consonant, it sounds similar to /ch/ of chat.

ㅇ + ㅏ + ㅊ = 앛
a t at

When ㅊ is the final consonant, it sounds similar to /t/ as in at.

차[cha] Tea/Car (동음이의어 Homonym)

차									

아침[a–chim] Morning

아	침								

닻[dat] Anchor

닻									

차	챠	처	쳐	초	쵸	추	츄	츠	치
차	챠	처	쳐	초	쵸	추	츄	츠	치
차	챠	처	쳐	초	쵸	추	츄	츠	치
차	챠	처	쳐	초	쵸	추	츄	츠	치
차	챠	처	쳐	초	쵸	추	츄	츠	치
앛	얓	엋	옃	옻	욫	웇	윷	읓	잋

CHAPTER
3

BASIC CONSONANTS 기본 자음
ㅋ 키읔 KIEUK

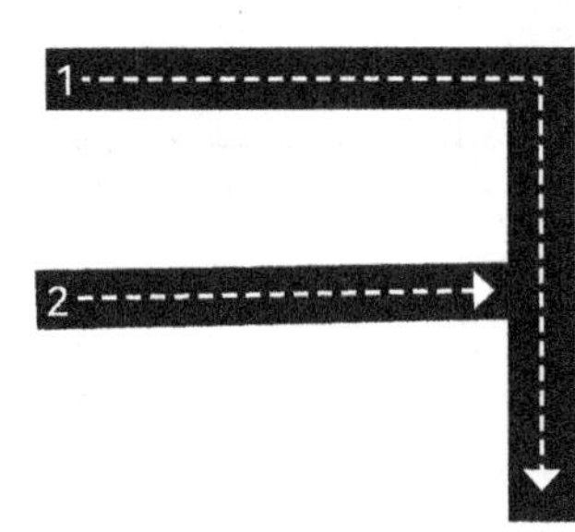

키읔 KI-EUK [k]

This consonant sounds similar to **K** of **K**etchup, **K**ind and Coo**k**.

ㅋ ㅋ ㅋ ㅋ ㅋ

ㅋ ㅋ ㅋ ㅋ ㅋ

ㅋ ㅋ ㅋ ㅋ ㅋ

ㅋ + ㅏ = 카
k a ka

ㅇ + ㅏ + ㅋ = 악
a k ak

ㅋ sounds like /k/ in both positions as the initial or final consonant.

ㅋ	ㅋ	ㅋ	ㅋ	ㅋ	ㅋ	ㅋ	ㅋ	ㅋ	ㅋ

코[ko] Nose

코									

칼[kal] Knife

칼									

부엌[bu-eok] Kitchen

부	엌								

카	캬	커	켜	코	쿄	쿠	큐	크	키
카	캬	커	켜	코	쿄	쿠	큐	크	키
카	캬	커	켜	코	쿄	쿠	큐	크	키
카	캬	커	켜	코	쿄	쿠	큐	크	키
카	캬	커	켜	코	쿄	쿠	큐	크	키
악	약	억	역	옥	욕	욱	육	윽	익

CHAPTER 3

BASIC CONSONANTS 기본 자음
ㅌ 티읕 TIEUT

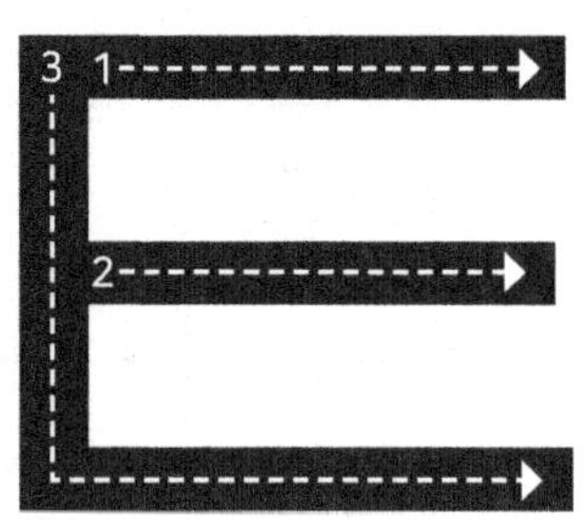

티읕 TI-EUT [t]

This consonant sounds similar to **T** of **T**oday, **T**iger, and Ca**t**.

ㅌ ㅌ ㅌ ㅌ ㅌ
ㅌ ㅌ ㅌ ㅌ ㅌ
ㅌ ㅌ ㅌ ㅌ ㅌ

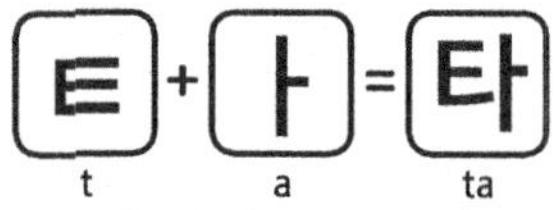

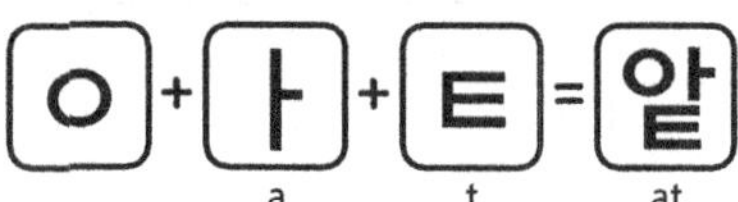

ㅌ sounds like /t/ in both positions as the initial or final consonant.

ㅌ	ㅌ	ㅌ	ㅌ	ㅌ	ㅌ	ㅌ	ㅌ	ㅌ	ㅌ

톱[top] Saw

톱									

타조[tajo] Ostrich

타	조								

밑[mit] Bottom

밑									

타	탸	터	텨	토	톼	투	튜	트	티
타	탸	터	텨	토	툐	투	튜	트	티
타	탸	터	텨	토	툐	투	튜	트	티
타	탸	터	텨	토	툐	투	튜	트	티
타	탸	터	텨	토	툐	투	튜	트	티
앝	얕	엍	옅	옽	욭	웉	윹	읕	잍

CHAPTER 3

BASIC CONSONANTS 기본 자음
ㅍ 피읖 PIEUP

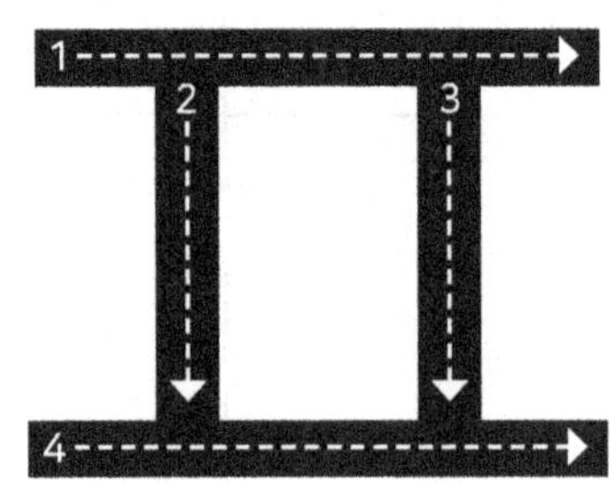

피읖 PI-EUP [p]

This consonant sounds similar to **P** of **P**ea, **P**anda, and A**pp**.

ㅍ ㅍ ㅍ ㅍ ㅍ

ㅍ ㅍ ㅍ ㅍ ㅍ

ㅍ ㅍ ㅍ ㅍ ㅍ

ㅍ + ㅏ = 파
p a pa

ㅇ + ㅏ + ㅍ = 앞
a p ap

ㅍ sounds like /p/ in both positions as the initial or final consonant.

ㅍ	ㅍ	ㅍ	ㅍ	ㅍ	ㅍ	ㅍ	ㅍ	ㅍ	ㅍ

앞[ap] Front

앞									

포도[podo] Grape

포	도								

파랑[pa-rang] Blue

파	랑								

파	퍄	퍼	펴	포	표	푸	퓨	프	피
파	퍄	퍼	펴	포	표	푸	퓨	프	피
파	퍄	퍼	펴	포	표	푸	퓨	프	피
파	퍄	퍼	펴	포	표	푸	퓨	프	피
파	퍄	퍼	펴	포	표	푸	퓨	프	피
앞	얖	엎	옆	옾	욮	웊	윺	읖	잎

CHAPTER 3

BASIC CONSONANTS 기본 자음
ㅎ 히읗 HIEUT

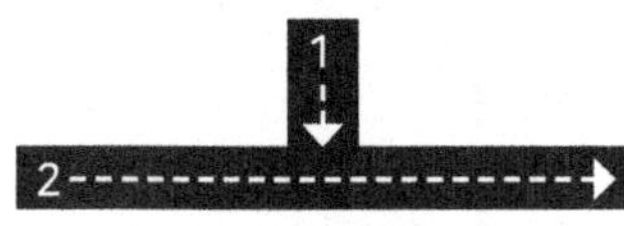

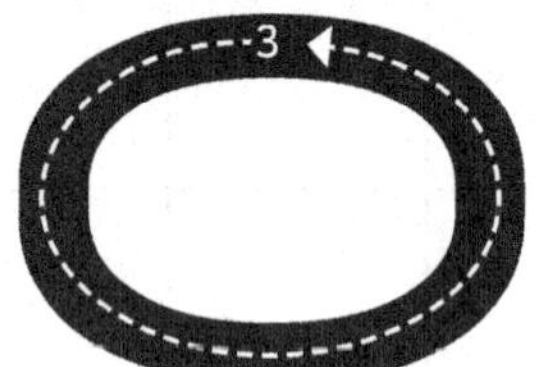

히읗 HI-EUT [h/t]

This consonant sounds similar to **H** of **H**ome and **H**appy.

ㅎ ㅎ ㅎ ㅎ ㅎ

ㅎ ㅎ ㅎ ㅎ ㅎ

ㅎ ㅎ ㅎ ㅎ ㅎ

ㅎ + ㅏ = 하
h a ha

When ㅎ is the initial consonant, it sounds similar to /h/ as in hi.

ㅇ + ㅏ + ㅎ = 앟
a t at

When ㅎ is the final consonant, it sounds similar to /t/ as in at.

ㅎ	ㅎ	ㅎ	ㅎ	ㅎ	ㅎ	ㅎ	ㅎ	ㅎ	ㅎ

하마 [ha–ma] Hippopotamus

하	마								

호박 [hobak] Pumpkin

호	박								

휴지 [hyuji] Toilet Paper

휴	지								

하	햐	허	혀	호	효	후	휴	흐	히
하	햐	허	혀	호	효	후	휴	흐	히
하	햐	허	혀	호	효	후	휴	흐	히
하	햐	허	혀	호	효	후	휴	흐	히
하	햐	허	혀	호	효	후	휴	흐	히
앟	얗	엏	옇	옿	욯	웋	윻	읗	잏

CHAPTER
3

Review 복습

1. Connect the Dots With the Matching Vowel's Sound.

ㄴ •	• g/k
ㅂ •	• n
ㅎ •	• d/t
ㄹ •	• r/l
ㄱ •	• m
ㅅ •	• b/p
ㅌ •	• s/t
ㅋ •	• -/ng
ㅊ •	• j/t
ㅁ •	• ch/t
ㅇ •	• k
ㄷ •	• t
ㅈ •	• p
ㅍ •	• h/t

2. Fill in the Blank Circles With the Basic Consonants in the Correct Order.

ㅁ

ㅇ

3. Word Search

기	윽	에	이	옹	디	리	을	자	을	뜯	비
미	음	디	장	비	읃	미	옴	시	읏	합	읍
벽	조	긋	라	시	읏	르	틈	뷰	항	니	톱
니	피	읍	니	울	치	일	키	읔	옷	은	듬
흔	지	읒	온	옷	읓	리	읃	비	이	히	륙
이	윽	상	키	기	욕	울	곳	옵	응	옿	보
옹	인	피	수	랑	초	억	히	읗	짙	잡	피
지	몇	읖	히	기	욕	보	티	달	공	리	읍
읒	른	튜	흫	찻	시	옷	은	승	섭	를	디
치	기	역	키	봄	굽	니	치	면	나	후	저
춪	약	안	윽	욕	걀	윽	읓	놈	디	덩	컬
너	래	면	흘	티	읕	꼼	경	묵	귿	숲	견

기역 리을 시옷 치읓 피읖

니은 미음 이응 키읔 히읗

디귿 비읍 지읒 티읕

Review 복습

4. Complete the Chart.

ㄱ 기역 [gi-yeok]	[ni-eun]	[di-geut]	ㄹ
[mi-eum]	ㅂ	[si-ot]	[i-eung]
ㅈ	[chi-eut]	ㅋ	[ti-eut]
[pi-eup]	ㅎ		

5. Write the Basic Vowels Under the Matching Pronunciation Three Times.

a	ya	eo	yeo	o	yo	u	yu	eu	i

6. Find 14 Basic Consonants.

7. Write the Basic Consonants Under the Matching Pronunciation Two Times.

g	n	d	r	m	b	s

ng	j	ch	k	t	p	h

CHAPTER 4

DOUBLE CONSONANTS 쌍자음

Hangeul has five double consonants: ㄲ, ㄸ, ㅃ, ㅆ, and ㅉ .

•Principle of **Laterally Attaching** (병서:byeongseo)
Double consonants are created via laterally attaching consonants.
For example, the first double consonant, ㄲ 쌍기역 ssang-giyeok, is composed of two giyeoks (ㄱ+ㄱ). 쌍기역(ssang-giyeok)'s 쌍(ssang) means double/pair.

•Pronunciation of Double Consonants
Double consonants are also called tense consonants because they articulate with stiffer and harder sounds than basic consonants. For example, 'Sin' has a tense and stiffer sound than 'shin'.

• ㄲ[kk], ㄸ[tt], ㅃ[pp]
There is no similar sound in English to give an example for these letters. ㄲ[kk],ㄸ[tt], and ㅃ[pp] have very close sounds to the Spanish alphabet C, T, and P. You can hear the sounds if you listen to the Spanish word 'capitalidad'. (Ca-Pi-Tal-li-dad[까-삐-딸-리-다-드])

• ㅆ[ss]
There are different sound references on siot and ssang-siot. Examples are all based on the letter S, but if you pay attention, ssang-siot's S has a tense sound.

ㅅ siot: **s**now, **s**low, **sh**ine, **sh**e   ㅆ ssang-siot: **s**ix, **s**un, **s**ick

• ㅉ[jj]
Ssang-jieut's closest resembling sound in English is in blackjack. The J of jack has a close sound to the letter ㅈ jieut. But, the J(kj) of blac**kj**ack has a similar sound to ㅉ ssang-jieut. (When pronouncing blackjack, it must be read jointly, not separately, like black jack.)

ㄲ

쌍기역
[ssang-giyeok]
kk
Final C: k of cook

ㄸ

쌍디귿
[ssang-digeut]
tt
Not used as Final C

ㅃ

쌍비읍
[ssang-bieup]
pp
Not used as Final C

쌍시옷
[ssang-siot]
ss
Final C: t of at

쌍지읒
[ssang-jieut]
jj
Not used as Final C

• Rule of **Becoming a Tense Sound**(경음화 gyeong-eum-hwa)
One of the Korean pronunciation rules is 'to become a tense sound'. When the batchim sound is [k],[t], or [p], and the following syllabic block's first sound is ㄱ,ㄷ,ㅂ,ㅅ, or ㅈ, the following sounds ㄱ,ㄷ,ㅂ,ㅅ, and ㅈ, become a tense sounds.

역기[yeok-gi] sounds like [역끼 yeok-kki]
접다[jeop-da] sounds like [접따 jeop-tta]

Final Consonant (batchim)		Following First Consonant		Following First Consonant Sound
[k] ㄱ, ㅋ, ㄲ				
[t] ㄷ, ㅌ, ㅅ, ㅆ, ㅈ, ㅊ	+	ㄱ,ㄷ,ㅂ,ㅅ,ㅈ	→	[ㄲ],[ㄸ],[ㅃ],[ㅆ],[ㅉ]
[p] ㅂ, ㅍ				

CHAPTER 4

DOUBLE CONSONANTS 쌍자음
ㄲ 쌍기역 SSANG-GIYEOK

ㄲ

쌍기역 SSANG-GI-YEOK [kk/k]
IPA[k͈] ㄱ+ㄱ Tense Consonant
No similar sound in English

ㄲ ㄲ ㄲ ㄲ ㄲ
ㄲ ㄲ ㄲ ㄲ ㄲ
ㄲ ㄲ ㄲ ㄲ ㄲ

ㄲ + ㅏ = 까
kk a kka

When ㄲ is the initial consonant, it sounds similar to /kk/.

ㅇ + ㅏ + ㄲ = 앆
a k ak

When ㄲ is the final consonant, it sounds similar to /k/ as in cook.

ㄲ	ㄲ	ㄲ	ㄲ	ㄲ	ㄲ	ㄲ	ㄲ	ㄲ	ㄲ

꽃 [kkot] Flower

꽃									

꿈 [kkum] Dream

꿈									

밖 [bak] Outside

밖									

까	꺄	꺼	껴	꼬	꾜	꾸	뀨	끄	끼
까	꺄	꺼	껴	꼬	꾜	꾸	뀨	끄	끼
까	꺄	꺼	껴	꼬	꾜	꾸	뀨	끄	끼
까	꺄	꺼	껴	꼬	꾜	꾸	뀨	끄	끼
까	꺄	꺼	껴	꼬	꾜	꾸	뀨	끄	끼
앆	얅	얶	엮	옦	욖	욲	윾	읶	읷

DOUBLE CONSONANTS 쌍자음
ㄸ 쌍디귿 SSANG-DIGEUT

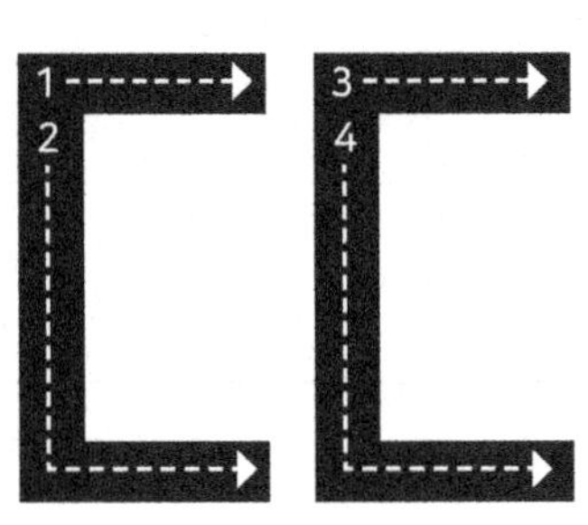

쌍디귿 SSANG-DI-GEUT [tt]
IPA[t͈] ㄷ+ㄷ Tense Consonant
No similar sound in English

ㄸ ㄸ ㄸ ㄸ ㄸ

ㄸ ㄸ ㄸ ㄸ ㄸ

ㄸ ㄸ ㄸ ㄸ ㄸ

ㄸ + ㅏ = 따
tt a tta

When ㄸ is the initial consonant, it sounds similar to /tt/.

ㅇ + ㅏ + ㄸ = X
a X X

Consonant ㄸ is not used as a final consonant.

ㄸ	ㄸ	ㄸ	ㄸ	ㄸ	ㄸ	ㄸ	ㄸ	ㄸ	ㄸ

똥 [ttong] Poop

똥									

딸기 [ttalgi] Strawberry

딸	기								

땅콩 [ttangkong] Peanut

땅	콩								

따	땨	떠	뗘	또	뚀	뚜	뜌	뜨	띠
따	땨	떠	뗘	또	뚀	뚜	뜌	뜨	띠
따	땨	떠	뗘	또	뚀	뚜	뜌	뜨	띠
따	땨	떠	뗘	또	뚀	뚜	뜌	뜨	띠
따	땨	떠	뗘	또	뚀	뚜	뜌	뜨	띠
따	땨	떠	뗘	또	뚀	뚜	뜌	뜨	띠

CHAPTER 4

DOUBLE CONSONANTS 쌍자음

ㅃ 쌍비읍 SSANG-BIEUP

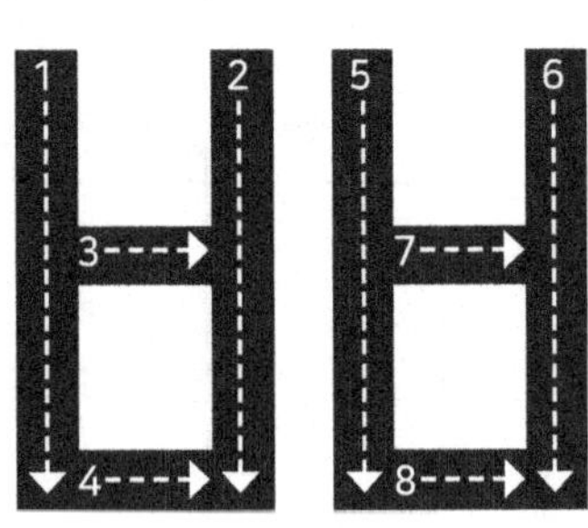

쌍비읍 SSANG-BI-EUP [pp]

IPA[p͈] ㅂ+ㅂ Tense Consonant

No similar sound in English

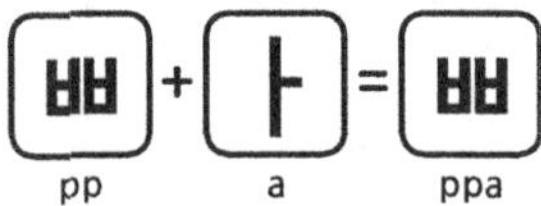

When ㅃ is the initial consonant, it sounds similar to /pp/.

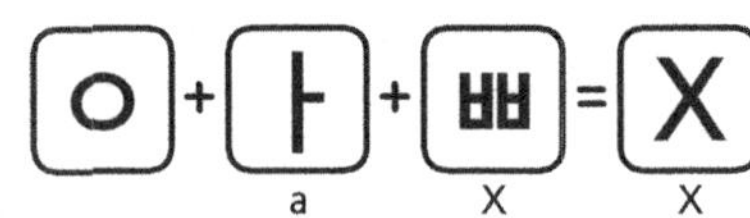

Consonant ㅃ is not used as a final consonant.

ㅃ	ㅃ	ㅃ	ㅃ	ㅃ	ㅃ	ㅃ	ㅃ	ㅃ	ㅃ

빵 [ppang] Bread

빵									

뿌리 [ppu-ri] Root

뿌	리								

빨강 [ppalgang] Red

빨	강								

빠	뺘	뻐	뼈	뽀	뾰	뿌	쀼	쁘	삐
빠	뺘	뻐	뼈	뽀	뾰	뿌	쀼	쁘	삐
빠	뺘	뻐	뼈	뽀	뾰	뿌	쀼	쁘	삐
빠	뺘	뻐	뼈	뽀	뾰	뿌	쀼	쁘	삐
빠	뺘	뻐	뼈	뽀	뾰	뿌	쀼	쁘	삐
빠	뺘	뻐	뼈	뽀	뾰	뿌	쀼	쁘	삐

CHAPTER 4

DOUBLE CONSONANTS 쌍자음
ㅆ 쌍시옷 SSANG-SIOT

쌍시옷 SSANG-SI-OT [ss/t]

IPA[s̪] ㅅ+ㅅ This consonant sounds similar to **S** of **S**ix, **S**un, and **S**ick. (*not* **S** in **S**lip, **S**kip)

ㅆ + ㅏ = 싸
ss a ssa

When ㅆ is the initial consonant, it sounds similar to /ss/ as in so.

ㅇ + ㅏ + ㅆ = 았
a t at

When ㅆ is the final consonant, it sounds similar to /t/ as in at.

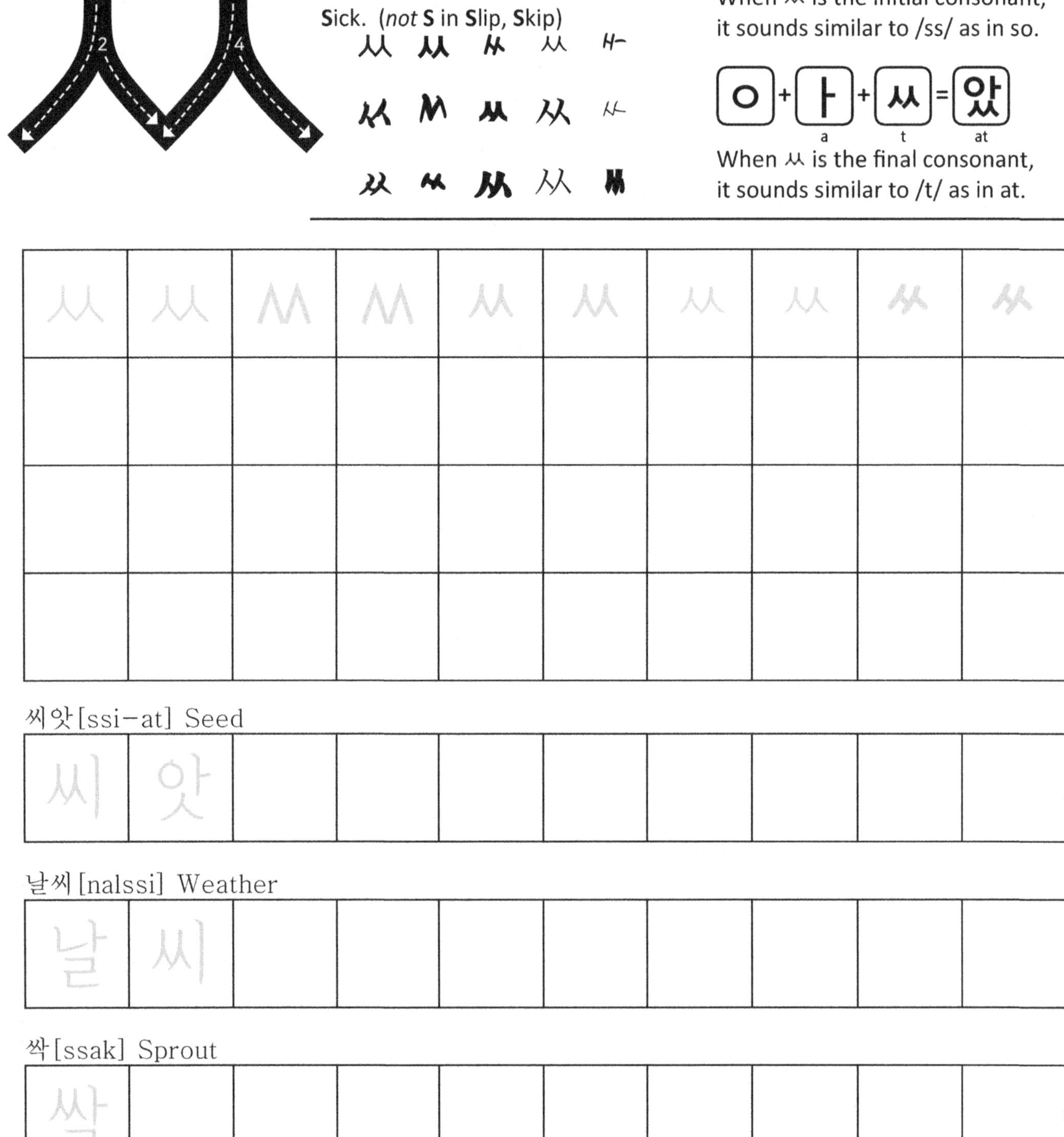

씨앗[ssi-at] Seed

날씨[nalssi] Weather

싹[ssak] Sprout

싸	쌰	써	쎠	쏘	쑈	쑤	쓔	쓰	씨
싸	쌰	써	쎠	쏘	쑈	쑤	쓔	쓰	씨
싸	쌰	써	쎠	쏘	쑈	쑤	쓔	쓰	씨
싸	쌰	써	쎠	쏘	쑈	쑤	쓔	쓰	씨
싸	쌰	써	쎠	쏘	쑈	쑤	쓔	쓰	씨
았	얐	었	였	옸	욨	웄	윴	읐	있

CHAPTER 4

DOUBLE CONSONANTS 쌍자음
ㅉ 쌍지읒 SSANG-JIEUT

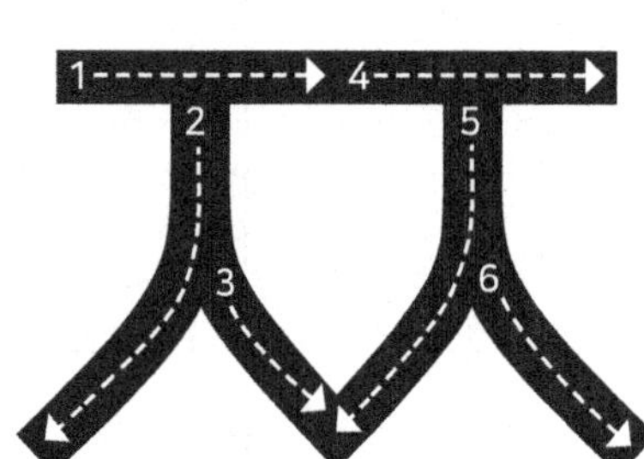

쌍지읒 SSANG-JI-EUT [jj]
IPA[t͡ɕ͈] ㅈ+ㅈ Tense Consonant
Similar sound to *kj* of Blac*k*jack
(not similar to J in Jack)

ㅉ ㅉ ㅉ ㅉ ㅉ
ㅉ ㅉ ㅉ ㅉ ㅉ
ㅉ ㅉ ㅉ ㅉ ㅉ

ㅉ + ㅏ = 짜
jj a a

When ㅉ is the initial consonant, it sounds similar to /jj/.

ㅇ + ㅏ + ㅉ = X
a X X

Consonant ㅉ is not used as a final consonant.

ㅉ	ㅉ	ㅉ	ㅉ	ㅉ	ㅉ	ㅉ	ㅉ	ㅉ	ㅉ

짝 [jjak] Pair

짝									

오른쪽 [oreunjjok] Right (Directional)

오	른	쪽							

찐빵 [jjinppang] Steamed Bun

찐	빵								

짜	쨔	쩌	쪄	쪼	쬬	쭈	쮸	쯔	찌
짜	쨔	쩌	쪄	쪼	쬬	쭈	쮸	쯔	찌
짜	쨔	쩌	쪄	쪼	쬬	쭈	쮸	쯔	찌
짜	쨔	쩌	쪄	쪼	쬬	쭈	쮸	쯔	찌
짜	쨔	쩌	쪄	쪼	쬬	쭈	쮸	쯔	찌
짜	쨔	쩌	쪄	쪼	쬬	쭈	쮸	쯔	찌

CHAPTER 4

Review 복습

Batchim Sound Chart : There Are Seven Sounds for the Final Consonants.

ㄱ[k]	ㄴ[n]	ㄷ[t]	ㄹ[l]	ㅁ[m]	ㅂ[p]	ㅇ[ng]
ㅋ ㄲ	ㄴ	ㄷ ㅅ ㅆ ㅈ ㅊ ㅌ ㅎ	ㄹ	ㅁ	ㅂ ㅍ	ㅇ

1. Choose the Correct Pronunciation for Each Word.

A. 옷장 (Wardrobe)
① [옷장] ② [옻장] ③ [오짱] ④ [옻짱] ⑤ [옫짱]

B. 깎다 (Peel , Cut, Carve, Lower)
① [깎다] ② [깍다] ③ [깎따] ④ [깍따] ⑤ [깓따]

C. 악어 (Crocodile, Alligator)
① [아거] ② [아꺼] ③ [악거] ④ [악꺼] ⑤ [악어]

D. 꽃다발 (Bouquet, Bunch of Flowers)
① [꽃다발] ② [꼳따발] ③ [꼳다발] ④ [꽃다빨] ⑤ [꼳따빨]

E. 덮개 (Cover, Lid)
① [덮개] ② [덥개] ③ [덥깨] ④ [덕깨] ⑤ [덕개]

F. 옆집 (House Next Door)
① [옆집] ② [엽집] ③ [엿집] ④ [엽찝] ⑤ [엿찝]

G. 어린이 (Children, Kids)
① [어린이] ② [어린니] ③ [어리니] ④ [얼리니] ⑤ [얼린니]

H. 책상 (Desk)
① [책상] ② [책쌍] ③ [챗쌍] ④ [챈쌍] ⑤ [챈상]

I. 입구 (Entrance)
① [입구] ② [익꾸] ③ [입꾸] ④ [익구] ⑤ [읶꾸]

J. 미역국 (Seaweed Soup)
① [미역국] ② [미역꾹] ③ [미엮꾹] ④ [미여꾹] ⑤ [믹엮꾹]

2. Write the Words in Hangeul.

Butterfly [na-bi]	Sky [ha-neul]	Bicycle [ja-jeon-geo]	Cat [go-yang-i]
나 비			
Today [o-neul]	**Now [ji-geum]**	**Puppy [gang-a-ji]**	**Cane [ji-pang-i]**

3. Write All of the Hangeul Consonants.

ㄱ	ㄲ	ㄴ	ㄷ	ㄸ	ㄹ	ㅁ	ㅂ	ㅃ	ㅅ
ㅆ	ㅇ	ㅈ	ㅉ	ㅊ	ㅋ	ㅌ	ㅍ	ㅎ	

CHAPTER

5 DIPHTHONGS (COMPLEX VOWELS) 복합 모음

Hangeul has 11 complex vowels: ㅐ, ㅒ, ㅔ, ㅖ, ㅘ, ㅙ, ㅚ, ㅝ ㅞ, ㅟ and ㅢ.
Complex Vowels are not new letters, but a combination of basic vowels.
For example, the complex vowel ㅐ is created by combining the two vowels ㅏ and ㅣ. Each letter in chapter 5 contains information on the origin of each complex vowel.

•Modern Korean pronunciation of complex vowels
Some complex vowels are difficult to distinguish via pronunciation.
To help with this issue, you should check the original letters that compose the complex vowels.

• ㅐ [ae], ㅔ [e]

For English speakers, these two letters' sounds are rather easy to distinguish.
Bad[배드] vs Bed[베드], Bat[뱃] vs Bet[벳]

•ㅙ[wae], ㅞ[we]

ㅙ[wae] starts with mouthing the ㅗ[o] sound, then is followed by the ㅐ[ae] sound. ㅞ[we] starts from the ㅜ[u] sound, then is followed by ㅔ[e] sound. Say aloud slowly **오애**[o-ae] or **우에**[u-e], then say them fast, thinking that you are combining them into a single sound.

•ㅚ[oe], ㅞ[we]

These two letters had different sounds in the past, but in modern Korean speech, most people pronounce them the same way. Nowadays, it is more common to read ㅚ[oe] the same as ㅞ[we].

•ㅢ[ui]

ㅢ[ui] does not have any similar sound in English. Read it as **으이**[eu-i] fast as if they are a single sound.

애[ae]
Bad
A of Bad

얘[yae]
Yam
Ya of Yam

에[e]
Bed
E of Bed

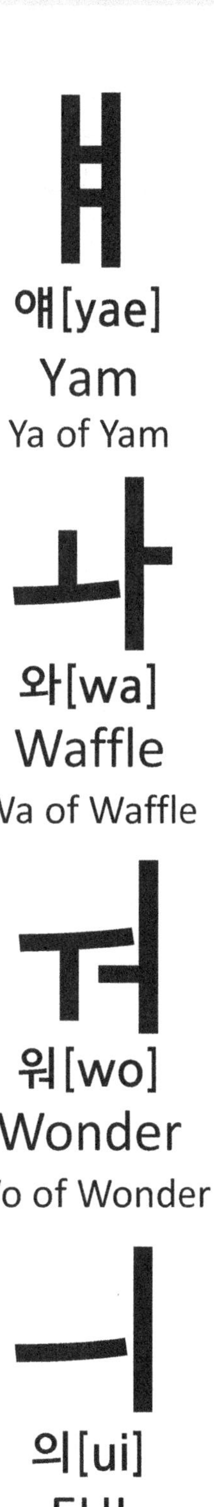

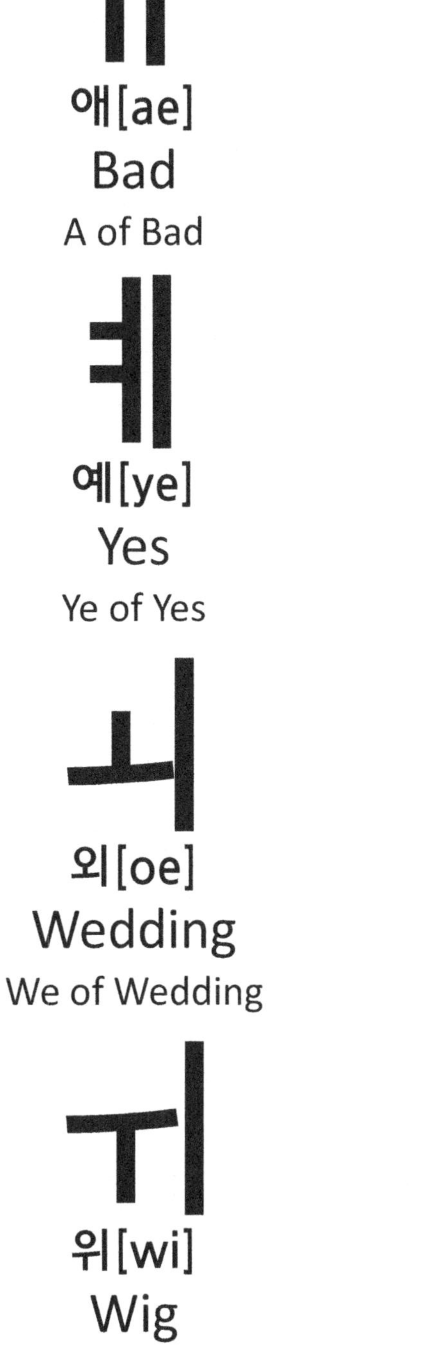

예[ye]
Yes
Ye of Yes

와[wa]
Waffle
Wa of Waffle

왜[wae]
Wagon
Wa of Wagon

외[oe]
Wedding
We of Wedding

워[wo]
Wonder
Wo of Wonder

웨[we]
Wedding
We of Wedding

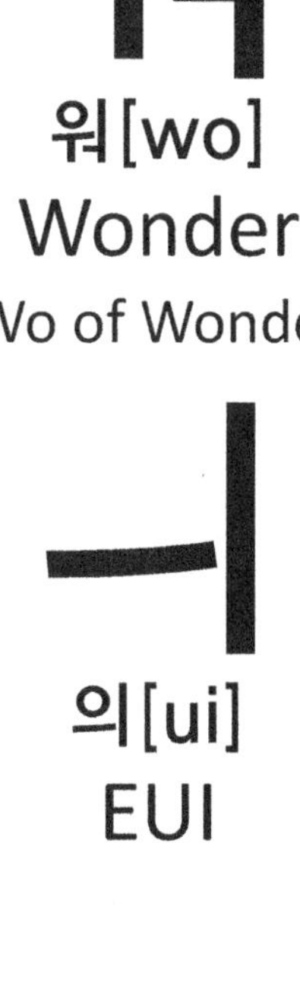

위[wi]
Wig
Wi of Wig

의[ui]
EUI

CHAPTER 5

DIPHTHONGS (COMPLEX VOWELS) 이중 모음
ㅐ 애 AE, ㅒ 얘 YAE

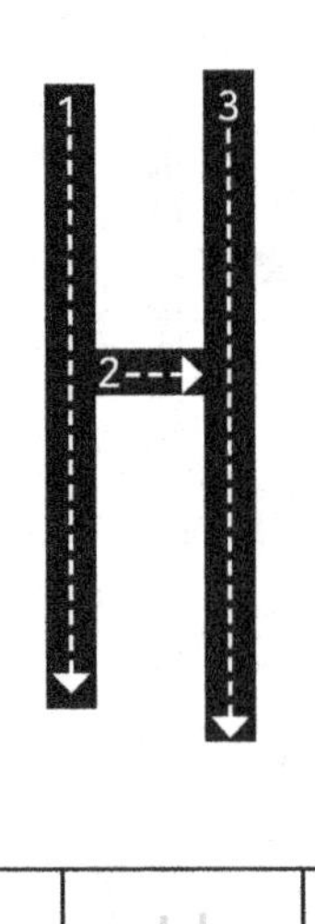

애 AE

ㅐ = ㅏ + ㅣ

ㅐ ㅐ ㅐ ㅐ ㅐ
ㅐ ㅐ ㅐ ㅐ ㅐ
ㅐ ㅐ ㅐ ㅐ ㅐ

ㅇ (c) + ㅐ (v, ae) = 애 (cv, ae)

ㅇ (c) + ㅐ (v, ae) + ㅇ (c, ng) = 앵 (cvc, aeng)

This vowel sounds similar to **A** of B**a**d, P**a**ss, and Perh**a**ps.

ㅐ	ㅐ	ㅐ	ㅐ	ㅐ	ㅐ	ㅐ	ㅐ	ㅐ	ㅐ
애	애	애	애	애	애	애	애	애	애

액자[aekjja] Frame

액	자								

채소[chae-so] Vegetable

채	소								

침대[chim-dae] Bed

침	대								

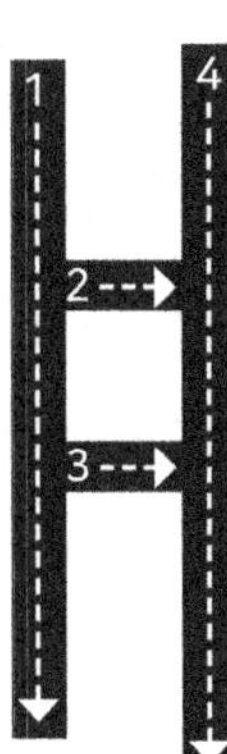

얘 YAE

ㅒ = ㅑ + ㅣ

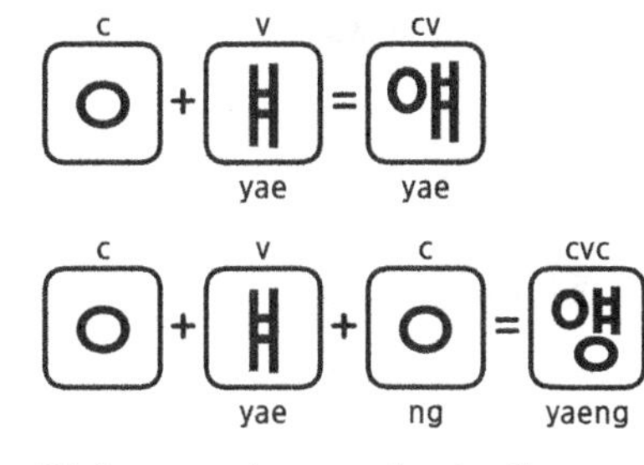

This vowel sounds similar to **Ya** of **Ya**m

얘[yae] This Child

걔[gyae] That Child ('that child' you have already been talking about in the conversation)

쟤[jyae] That Child ('that child' in the distance from the person who talks or listens)

DIPHTHONGS (COMPLEX VOWELS) 이중 모음
ㅔ 에 E, ㅖ 예 YE

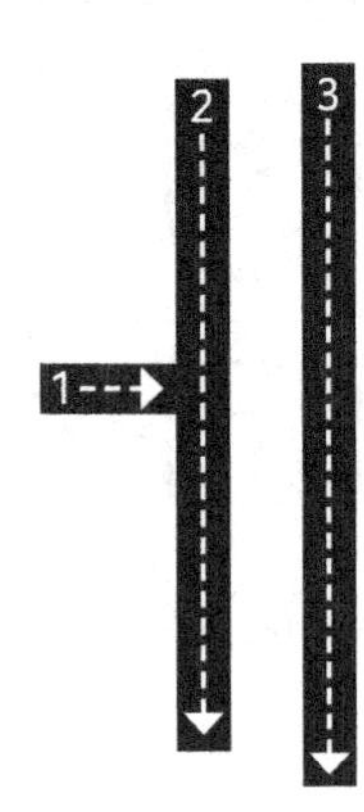

에 E

ㅔ = ㅓ + ㅣ

ㅔ ㅔ ㅔ ㅔ ㅔ
ㅔ ㅔ ㅔ ㅔ ㅔ
ㅔ ㅔ ㅔ ㅔ ㅔ

ㅇ (c) + ㅔ (v, e) = 에 (cv, e)

ㅇ (c) + ㅔ (v, e) + ㅇ (c, ng) = 엥 (cvc, eng)

This vowel sounds similar to **E** of B**e**d and P**e**n.

ㅔ	ㅔ	ㅔ	ㅔ	ㅔ	ㅔ	ㅔ	ㅔ	ㅔ	ㅔ
에	에	에	에	에	에	에	에	에	에

게 [ge] Crab

게									

넥타이 [nekta-i] Necktie

넥	타	이							

애벌레 [ae-beolle] Caterpillar

애	벌	레							

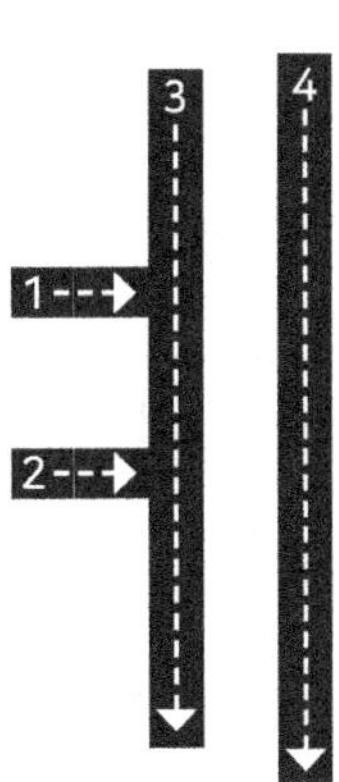

예 YE

ㅖ = ㅕ + ㅣ

ㅖ ㅖ ㅖ ㅖ ㅖ
ㅖ ㅖ ㅖ ㅖ ㅖ
ㅖ ㅖ ㅖ ㅖ ㅖ

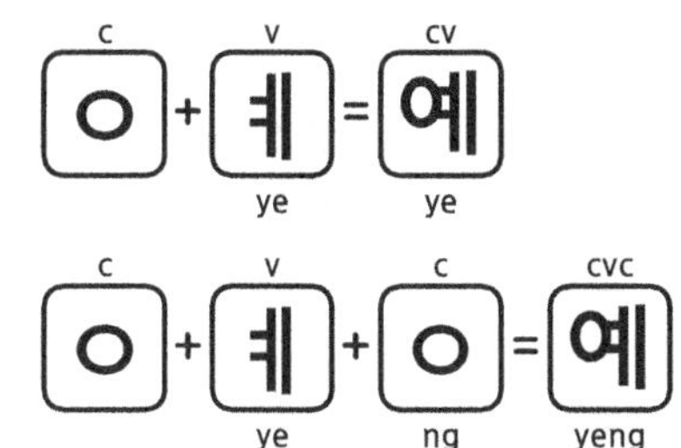

This vowel sounds similar to **YE** of **Ye**s and **Ye**ll.

ㅖ	ㅖ	ㅖ	ㅖ	ㅖ	ㅖ	ㅖ	ㅖ	ㅖ	ㅖ
예	예	예	예	예	예	예	예	예	예

계단[gyedan] Stairs

계	단								

시계[si-gye] Clock

시	계								

체중계[chejung-gye] Scale(for body weight)

체	중	계							

CHAPTER 5

DIPHTHONGS (COMPLEX VOWELS) 이중 모음
ㅘ 와 WA, ㅙ 왜 WAE

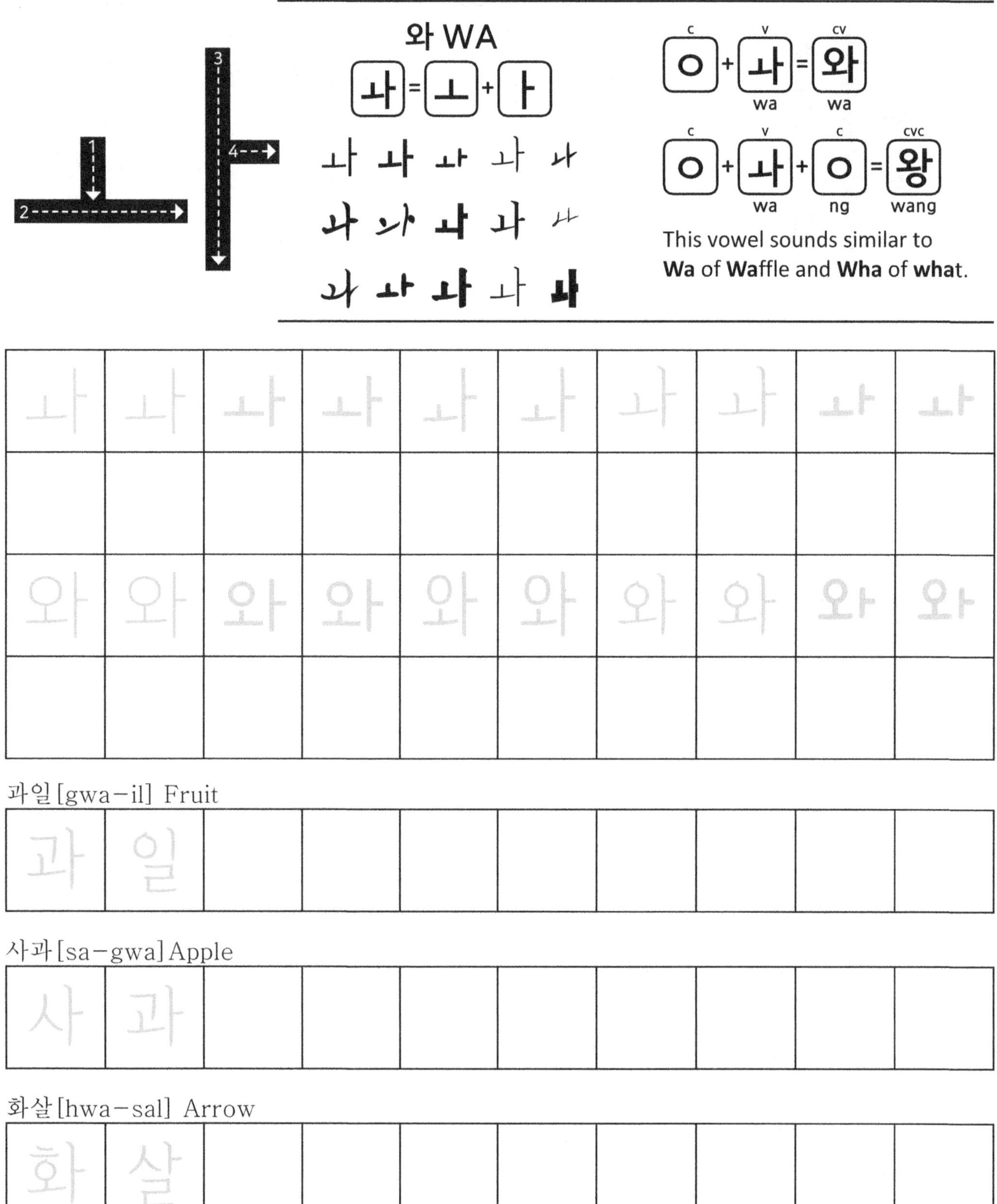

This vowel sounds similar to **Wa** of **Wa**ffle and **Wha** of **wha**t.

과일 [gwa–il] Fruit

과 일

사과 [sa–gwa] Apple

사 과

화살 [hwa–sal] Arrow

화 살

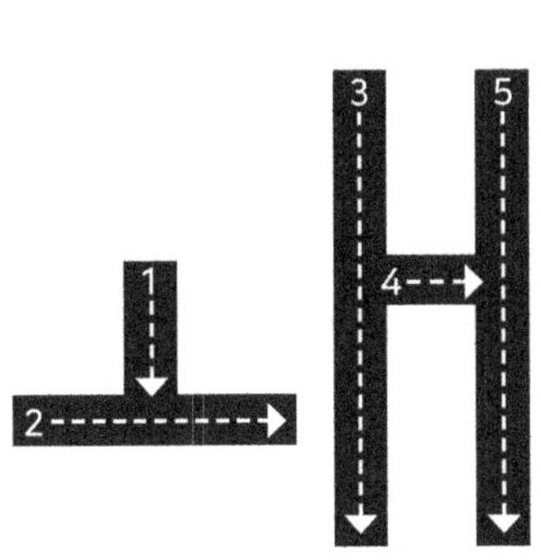

왜 WAE

ㅙ = ㅗ + ㅐ

ㅙ ㅙ ㅙ ㅙ ㅙ
ㅙ ㅙ ㅙ ㅙ ㅙ
ㅙ ㅙ ㅙ ㅙ ㅙ

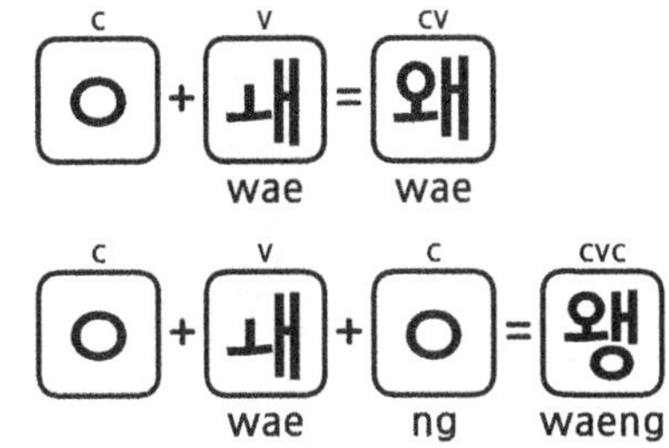

This vowel sounds similar to **WA** of **wa**gon and s**wa**g.

ㅙ	ㅙ	ㅙ	ㅙ	ㅙ	ㅙ	ㅙ	ㅙ	ㅙ	ㅙ
왜	왜	왜	왜	왜	왜	왜	왜	왜	왜

돼지 [dwaeji] Pig

돼	지								

인쇄 [inswae] Print

인	쇄								

횃불 [hwaetppul] Torch

횃	불								

DIPHTHONGS (COMPLEX VOWELS) 이중 모음
ㅚ 외 OE, ㅝ 워 WO

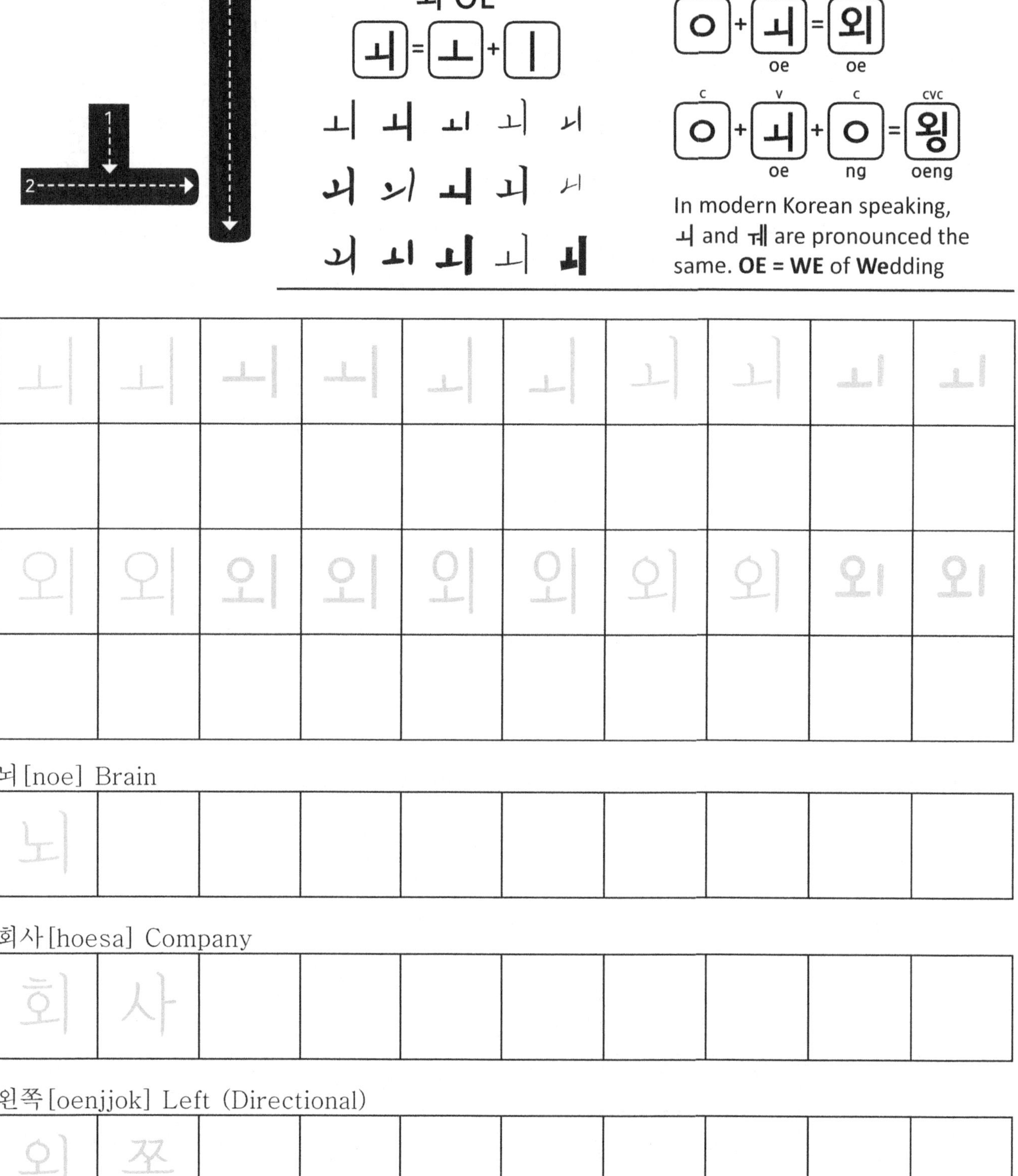

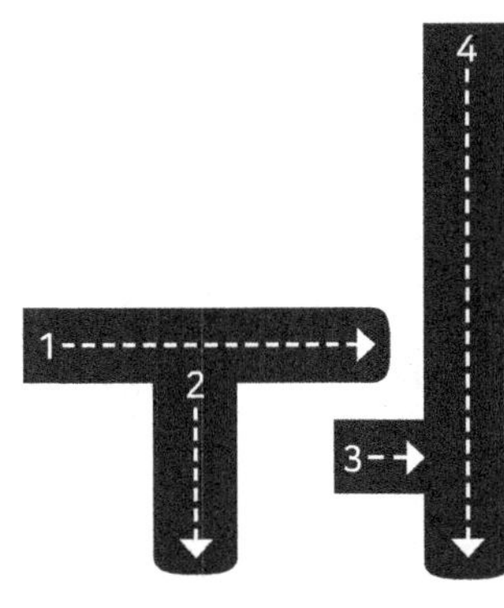

워 WO

ㅝ = ㅜ + ㅓ

ㅝ ㅝ ㅝ ㅝ ㅝ
ㅝ ㅝ ㅝ ㅝ ㅝ
ㅝ ㅝ ㅝ ㅝ ㅝ

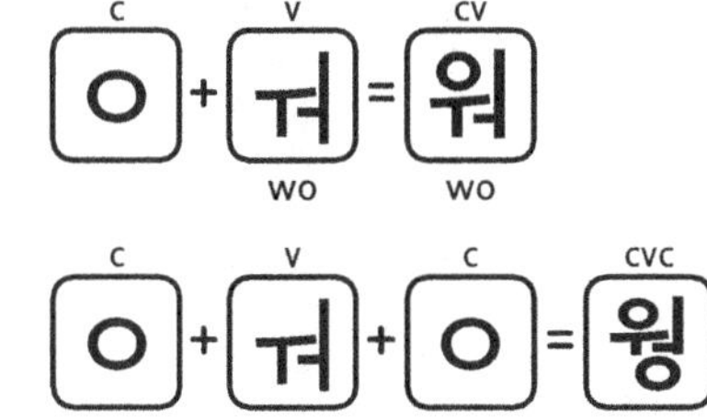

This vowel sounds similar to **WO** of **Wo**nder.

ㅝ	ㅝ	ㅝ	ㅝ	ㅝ	ㅝ	ㅝ	ㅝ	ㅝ	ㅝ
워	워	워	워	워	워	워	워	워	워

병원 [byeong-won] Hospital

병	원								

유치원 [yuchi-won] Kindergarten

유	치	원							

원숭이 [wonsung-i] Monkey

원	숭	이							

CHAPTER 5

DIPHTHONGS (COMPLEX VOWELS) 이중 모음
ㅞ 웨 WE, ㅟ 위 WI

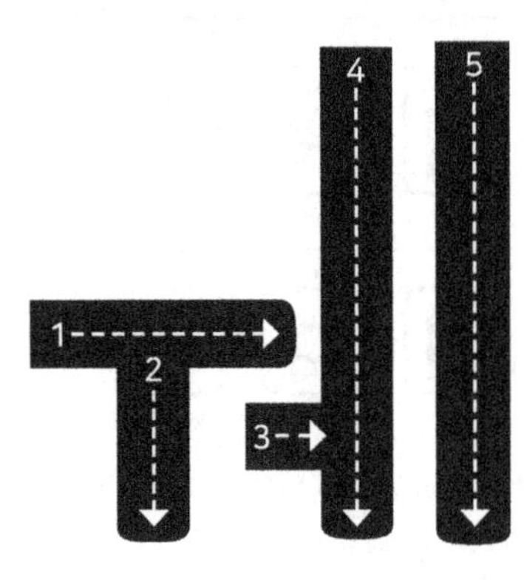

웨 WE

ㅞ = ㅜ + ㅔ

ㅞ ㅞ ㅞ ㅞ ㅞ
ㅞ ㅞ ㅞ ㅞ ㅞ
ㅞ ㅞ ㅞ ㅞ ㅞ

ㅇ (c) + ㅞ (v, we) = 웨 (cv, we)

ㅇ (c) + ㅞ (v, we) + ㅇ (c, ng) = 웽 (cvc, weng)

This vowel sounds similar to **WE** of **We**dding and **We**b.

ㅞ	ㅞ	ㅞ	ㅞ	ㅞ	ㅞ	ㅞ	ㅞ	ㅞ	ㅞ
웨	웨	웨	웨	웨	웨	웨	웨	웨	웨

궤도[gwedo] Orbital Path

궤	도								

궤짝[gwejjak] Wooden Crate

궤	짝								

스웨터[seuweteo] Sweater

스	웨	터							

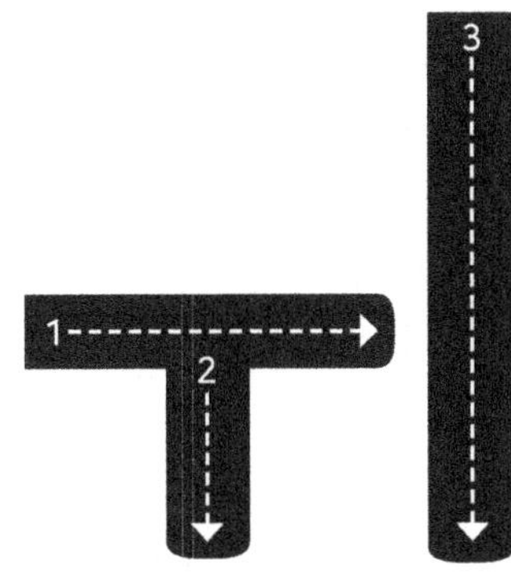

위 WI

ㅟ = ㅜ + ㅣ

ㅇ + ㅟ = 위
c v cv
wi wi

ㅇ + ㅟ + ㅇ = 윙
c v c cvc
wi ng wing

This vowel sounds similar to **WI** of **Wi**n and **Wi**ng.

ㅟ	ㅟ	ㅟ	ㅟ	ㅟ	ㅟ	ㅟ	ㅟ	ㅟ	ㅟ
위	위	위	위	위	위	위	위	위	위

가위[ga-wi] Scissors

가	위								

바퀴[ba-kwi] Wheel

바	퀴								

다람쥐[da-ramjwi] Chipmunk

다	람	쥐							

CHAPTER 5

DIPHTHONGS (COMPLEX VOWELS) 이중 모음
ㅢ 의 UI

의 UI

ㅢ = ㅡ + ㅣ

ㅇ + ㅢ = 의
c + v (ui) = cv (ui)

ㅇ + ㅢ + ㅇ = 읭
c + v (ui) + c (ng) = cvc (uing)

There is no similar sound in English. Say [eu] and [i] together as if they are one sound (eui).

ㅢ	ㅢ	ㅢ	ㅢ	ㅢ	ㅢ	ㅢ	ㅢ	ㅢ	ㅢ
의	의	의	의	의	의	의	의	의	의

의견[uigyeon] Opinion

의	견								

의사[uisa] Doctor

의	사								

의자[uija] Chair

의	자								

Review All of the Hangeul Letters

Dictionary Order of the Korean Vowels :

ㅏ, ㅐ, ㅑ, ㅒ, ㅓ, ㅔ, ㅕ, ㅖ, ㅗ, ㅘ, ㅙ, ㅚ, ㅛ, ㅜ, ㅝ, ㅞ, ㅟ, ㅠ, ㅡ, ㅢ, ㅣ

Dictionary Order of the Korean Consonants :

ㄱ, ㄲ, ㄴ, ㄷ, ㄸ, ㄹ, ㅁ, ㅂ, ㅃ, ㅅ, ㅆ, ㅇ, ㅈ, ㅉ, ㅊ, ㅋ, ㅌ, ㅍ, ㅎ

아	애	야	얘	어	에	여	예	오	와
왜	외	요	우	워	웨	위	유	으	의
이	가	까	나	다	따	라	마	바	빠
사	싸	아	자	짜	차	카	타	파	하

Batchim Sound Chart : There Are Seven Sounds for the Final Consonants.

ㄱ[k]	ㄴ[n]	ㄷ[t]	ㄹ[l]	ㅁ[m]	ㅂ[p]	ㅇ[ng]
ㅋ ㄲ	ㄴ	ㄷ ㅅ ㅆ ㅈ ㅊ ㅌ ㅎ	ㄹ	ㅁ	ㅂ ㅍ	ㅇ

CHAPTER 5

Review 복습

1. Connect the Dots With the Matching Sound and Example.

Vowel	Sound	Example
ㅖ •	• ae •	• **We**dding
ㅢ •	• yae •	• **Wi**g
ㅐ •	• e •	• **Ya**m
ㅘ •	• ye •	• **Ye**s
ㅞ •	• wa •	• Bed
ㅟ •	• wae •	• Bad
ㅙ •	• oe •	• **Wa**ffle
ㅔ •	• wo •	• **Eui**
ㅒ •	• we •	• **Wa**gon
ㅚ •	• wi •	• **Wo**nder
ㅝ •	• ui •	

2. Fill in the Blank Circles With the Vowels in the Dictionary Order.

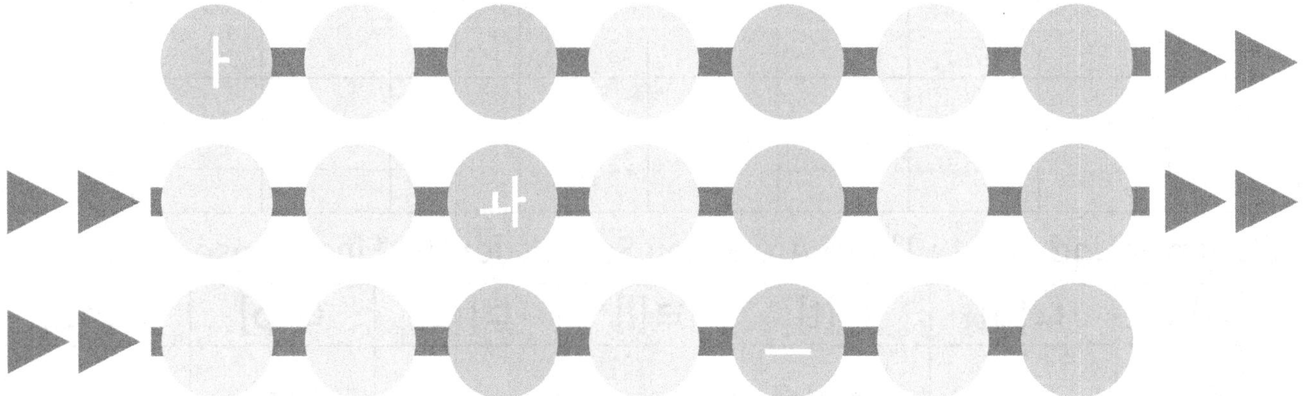

3. Find the 11 Complex Vowels from Chapter 5.

4. Write the Basic Vowels Under the Matching Pronunciation Five Times.

ae	yae	e	ye	wa	wae	oe	wo	we	wi	ui

CHAPTER 6 DOUBLE FINAL CONSONANTS 겹받침

There are 11 special final consonants called double final consonants; ㄳ, ㄵ, ㄶ, ㄺ, ㄻ, ㄼ, ㄽ, ㄾ, ㄿ, ㅀ, ㅄ. These letters are only used as final consonants, and are composed of two different basic consonants; ㄱ+ㅅ→ㄳ. 'The Basic Pronunciation of the Double Final Consonants Chart' below shows their sounds when they are written alone without any following syllabic block. Some letters sound like the first letter of the double final consonants, and some sound like the second letter. For example, 몫 sounds like [목], but 앎 sounds like [암]. But, there are more steps to consider before pronouncing words made of multiple syllabic blocks.

Let's look at some examples; 앉, 앉아, and 앉다.

앉 [안, an] : ㄵ sounds as ㄴ[nieun], and the ㅈ[jieut] is silent.

앉아 [안자, anja] : ㄵ's ㄴ[nieun] sound stays in the first syllabic block, and the ㅈ[jieut] sound links to the following syllabic block's consonant ㅇ[ieung].

앉다 [안따, antta] : ㄵ's ㄴ[nieun] sound stays in the first syllabic block, and ㅈ[jieut] affects the following syllabic block's consonant ㄷ[digeut]. ㄷ[digeut] will sound like ㄸ[ssang-digeut] because of the rule of become a tense sound.

The Basic Pronunciation of the Double Final Consonants Chart

ㄱ[k]	ㄴ[n]	ㄷ[t]	ㄹ[l]	ㅁ[m]	ㅂ[p]	ㅇ[ng]
ㄳ ㄺ	ㄵ ㄶ		ㄼ ㄽ ㄾ ㅀ	ㄻ	ㄿ ㅄ	

ㄳ

기역시옷
[gi-yeok-si-ot]

ㄵ

니은지읒
[ni-eun-ji-eut]

ㄶ

니은히읗
[ni-eun-hi-eut]

ㄺ

리을기역
[ri-eul-gi-yeok]

ㄻ

리을미음
[ri-eul-mi-eum]

ㄼ

리을비읍
[ri-eul-bi-eup]

ㄽ

리을시옷
[ri-eul-si-ot]

ㄾ

리을티읕
[ri-eul-ti-eut]

ㄿ

리을피읖
[ri-eul-pi-eup]

ㅀ

리을히읗
[ri-eul-hi-eut]

ㅄ

비읍시옷
[bi-eup-si-ot]

CHAPTER 6

DOUBLE FINAL CONSONANTS 겹받침

몫[mok] Share, Portion / Role, Duty

몫									

앉다[antta] Sit

앉	다								

끊다[kkeunta] Cut / Break Off, Cut Off / Stop, Quit

끊	다								

읽다[iktta] Read

읽	다								

앎[am] Knowledge, Wisdom

앎									

넓다[neoltta] Broad, Wide

넓	다								

외곬[oegol] Single Way

외	곬								

핥다[haltta] Lick

핥	다								

읊다[euptta] Recite

끓다[kkeulta] Boil

없다[eobtta] Non-Existent, Lacking

닭[dak] Chicken

흙[heuk] Soil

삶[sam] Life

옳다[olta] Right, Correct

값[gap] Price, Payment

CHAPTER 7

Review

Practice reading with these borrowed words that are used in Korea, and guess what each word means. (EX: **토마토** means tomato in English).

0. 토마토 to-ma-to
1. 키위
2. 프랑스
3. 콜라
4. 캐나다
5. 와인
6. 라마
7. 피아노
8. 바나나
9. 고릴라
10. 스페인
11. 모델
12. 커피
13. 기타
14. 브라질
15. 피클
16. 퍼즐
17. 파인애플
18. 멕시코
19. 아보카도
20. 칵테일
21. 휠체어
22. 이탈리아
23. 블루베리
24. 주스
25. 바이올린
26. 스위스
27. 코알라
28. 드레스
29. 라임
30. 케첩
31. 버스

32. 컴퓨터
33. 침팬지
34. 오디오
35. 복싱
36. 소파
37. 뮤지컬
38. 판다
39. 로열티
40. 하프
41. 앨범
42. 샴푸
43. 노하우
44. 햄스터
45. 도넛
46. 피자
47. 사우나
48. 햄버거
49. 인테리어
50. 캥거루
51. 스피커
52. 훌라후프
53. 마사지
54. 튤립
55. 초콜릿
56. 시스템
57. 펭귄
58. 디자인
59. 지그재그
60. 네온사인
61. 골키퍼
62. 박테리아
63. 카멜레온

Day 1

10 Days of Review

	ㅏ	ㅑ	ㅓ	ㅕ	ㅗ	ㅛ	ㅜ	ㅠ	ㅡ	ㅣ
ㄱ		갸								
ㄴ										
ㄷ										
ㄹ										
ㅁ						묘				
ㅂ										
ㅅ										
ㅇ										
ㅈ									즈	
ㅊ										
ㅋ										
ㅌ										
ㅍ										
ㅎ										

Fruit 과일

(If you need the romanized pronunciation, go to page 112.)

Tangerine

귤											

Strawberry

딸	기										

Peach

복	숭	아									

Apple

사	과										

Pomegranate

석	류										

Watermelon

수	박										

Dragon Fruit

용	과										

Plum

자	두										

Grapefruit

자	몽										

Grape

포	도										

10 Days of Review

	ㅐ	ㅒ	ㅔ	ㅖ	ㅘ	ㅙ	ㅚ	ㅝ	ㅞ	ㅟ	ㅢ
ㄱ											
ㄴ											
ㄷ			데								
ㄹ											
ㅁ											
ㅂ											
ㅅ							쇠				
ㅇ											
ㅈ											
ㅊ											
ㅋ											
ㅌ											
ㅍ										퓌	
ㅎ											

Vegetable 채소

(If you need the romanized pronunciation, go to page 112.)

Eggplant

가지

Potato

감자

Carrot

당근

Mushroom

버섯

Lettuce

상추

Onion

양파

Cucumber

오이

Corn

옥수수

Bell Pepper

피망

Pumpkin

호박

	ㄲ	ㄸ	ㅃ	ㅆ	ㅉ		ㄲ	ㄸ	ㅃ	ㅆ	ㅉ
ㅏ						ㅚ					
ㅐ						ㅛ					
ㅑ						ㅜ					
ㅒ						ㅝ					
ㅓ						ㅞ					
ㅔ						ㅟ					
ㅕ						ㅠ					
ㅖ						ㅡ					
ㅗ						ㅢ					
ㅘ						ㅣ					
ㅙ											

Days of the Week 요일

(If you need the romanized pronunciation, go to page 112.)

One Week

일	주	일									

Day of the Week (Ex: What "day of the week" is it? Expected M–S not a date)

요	일										

Monday

월	요	일									

Tuesday

화	요	일									

Wednesday

수	요	일									

Thursday

목	요	일									

Friday

금	요	일									

Saturday

토	요	일									

Sunday

일	요	일									

One Day

하	루										

Day 4

10 Days of Review

	ㅏㄱ	ㅑㄴ	ㅓㄴ	ㅕㄹ	ㅗㅁ	ㅗㅂ	ㅗㅅ	ㅠㅇ	ㅜㅈ	ㅣㅊ
ㄱ										
ㄴ										
ㄷ			던							
ㄹ								룽		
ㅁ										
ㅂ										
ㅅ										
ㅇ										
ㅈ					좀					
ㅊ										
ㅋ										
ㅌ										
ㅍ										
ㅎ										

Color 색깔

(If you need the romanized pronunciation, go to page 112.)

Red 빨강 = Red Color 빨간색

Orange 주황 = Orange Color 주황색

Yellow 노랑 = Yellow Color 노란색

Green 초록 = Green Color 초록색

Blue 파랑 = Blue Color 파랑색

Pink 분홍 = Pink Color 분홍색

Purple 보라 = Purple Color 보라색

White 하양 = White Color 하얀색, 흰색, 백색

Gray 회색 = Gray Color 회색

Black 검정 = Black Color 검정색

	ㅏㅋ	ㅑㅌ	ㅓㅍ	ㅕㅎ	ㅗㄱ	ㅛㄴ	ㅜㄹ	ㅠㅁ	ㅡㅂ	ㅣㅅ
ㄱ					곡					
ㄴ										
ㄷ							둘			
ㄹ										
ㅁ										
ㅂ										
ㅅ										
ㅇ										
ㅈ										짓
ㅊ										
ㅋ										
ㅌ										
ㅍ										
ㅎ										

Country 국가

(If you need the romanized pronunciation, go to page 112.)

Germany

독	일										

Mexico

멕	시	코									

The United States of America

미	국										

United Kingdom

영	국										

India

인	도										

Japan

일	본										

China

중	국										

Canada

캐	나	다									

Thailand

태	국										

Australia

호	주										

10 Days of Review

	ㅏ	ㅑ	ㅓ	ㅕ	ㅗ	ㅛ	ㅜ	ㅠ	ㅡ	ㅣ
ㄱ										
ㄴ										
ㄷ										
ㄹ										
ㅁ										
ㅂ										
ㅅ										
ㅇ										
ㅈ										
ㅊ										
ㅋ										
ㅌ										
ㅍ										
ㅎ										

Republic of Korea 대한민국

(If you need the romanized pronunciation, go to page 112.)

Republic of Korea; Official and Formal Name of Korea

대	한	민	국								

Abbreviation of 대한민국; Casual Form

한	국										

The National Flag of Korea

태	극	기									

Korean Letters (Korean Alphabet)

한	글										

Korean Language

한	국	어									

Korean (Person)

한	국	인									

Traditional Korean Clothes

한	복										

South Korea • North Korea

남	한	•	북	한							

Korea's Name From 1392 to 1910

조	선										

Korea's Name From 918 to 1392

고	려										

10 Days of Review

	ㅐ	ㅒ	ㅔ	ㅖ	ㅘ	ㅙ	ㅚ	ㅝ	ㅞ	ㅟ	ㅢ
ㄱ											
ㄴ											
ㄷ											
ㄹ											
ㅁ											
ㅂ											
ㅅ											
ㅇ											
ㅈ											
ㅊ											
ㅋ											
ㅌ											
ㅍ											
ㅎ											

Shape 모양

(If you need the romanized pronunciation, go to page 112.)

Circle 동그라미 = 원(Sino-Korean)

동 그 라 미

Triangle

세 모

Triangle(Sino-Korean)

삼 각 형

Square

네 모

Square (Sino-Korean) (오각형 Pentagon, 육각형 Hexagon)

사 각 형

Diamond

마 름 모

Star Shape

별 모 양

Semi-Circle

반 원

Oval

타 원

Cylinder

원 기 둥

10 Days of Review

	ㄲ	ㄸ	ㅃ	ㅆ	ㅉ		ㄲ	ㄸ	ㅃ	ㅆ	ㅉ
ㅏ						ㅚ					
ㅐ						ㅛ					
ㅑ						ㅜ					
ㅒ						ㅝ					
ㅓ						ㅞ					
ㅔ						ㅟ					
ㅕ						ㅠ					
ㅖ						ㅡ					
ㅗ						ㅢ					
ㅘ						ㅣ					
ㅙ											

Transportation 탈 것

(If you need the romanized pronunciation, go to page 113.)

Motor Vehicle/Car; Abbreviation = 차

자	동	차									

Train

기	차										

Subway

지	하	철									

Bus

버	스										

Bicycle

자	전	거									

Ship

배											

Airplane

비	행	기									

Fire Engine

소	방	차									

Ambulance

구	급	차									

Police Car

경	찰	차									

10 Days of Review

	ㅏ	ㅑ	ㅓ	ㅕ	ㅗ	ㅛ	ㅜ	ㅠ	ㅡ	ㅣ
ㄱ										
ㄴ										
ㄷ										
ㄹ										
ㅁ										
ㅂ										
ㅅ										
ㅇ										
ㅈ										
ㅊ										
ㅋ										
ㅌ										
ㅍ										
ㅎ										

The Numbers 숫자 (Sino-Korean Numbers)

(If you need the romanized pronunciation, go to page 113.)

One 一

일

Two 二

이

Three 三

삼

Four 四

사

Five 五

오

Six 六

육

Seven 七

칠

Eight 八

팔

Nine 九

구

Ten 十

십

10 Days of Review

	a	ya	eo	yeo	o	yo	u	yu	eu	i
g	가									
n										
d										
r										
m							무			
b										
s										
-/ng										
j										
ch										
k										
t										
p										
h										

The Numbers 숫자 (Native Korean Numbers)

(If you need the romanized pronunciation, go to page 113.)

One

하 나

Two

둘

Three

셋

Four

넷

Five

다 섯

Six

여 섯

Seven

일 곱

Eight

여 덟

Nine

아 홉

Ten

열

A Answers

Ch 2 - 1

ㅏ	•—•	a	•—•	**Avocado**
ㅑ	•—•	ya	•—•	**Yard**
ㅓ	•—•	eo	•—•	**O**nion
ㅕ	•—•	yeo	•—•	**You**ng
ㅗ	•—•	o	•—•	**O**n
ㅛ	•—•	yo	•—•	**Yo-Yo**
ㅜ	•—•	u	•—•	M**oo**n
ㅠ	•—•	yu	•—•	**You**
ㅡ	•—•	eu	•—•	g**eu**rin
ㅣ	•—•	i	•—•	**I**nn

Ch 2 - 2

ㅏ ㅑ ㅓ ㅕ ㅗ

Ch 2 - 3

0) [yo-yo]
1) [yeong]
2) [i]
3) [o]
4) [o-i]
5) [yeo-u]
6) [u-yu]
7) [a-i]

Ch 2 - 4

ᅱ	下	p	ᄝ	ㅓ	i	**ㅣ**	ㅖ	こ	ب
天	ㅐ	ζ	工	**ㅛ**	く	川	ㅚ	**ㅕ**	f
o	**ㅏ**	ᅙᅙ	ヘ	ㅖ	ㅚ	土	**ㅡ**	ㅝ	上
ㅜ	j	ㅠ	ㅘ	ん	**ㅓ**	d	△	ㄴ	**ㅠ**
ㅒ	い	二	**ㅑ**	I	ٺ	ㅔ	**ㅗ**	y	ㅙ

Ch 2 - 5

a	ya	eo	yeo	o	yo	u	yu	eu	i
아	야	어	여	오	요	우	유	으	이

Ch 3 - 1

ㄱ	•—•	g/k	ㅇ	•—•	-/ng
ㄴ	•—•	n	ㅈ	•—•	j/t
ㄷ	•—•	d/t	ㅊ	•—•	ch/t
ㄹ	•—•	r/l	ㅋ	•—•	k
ㅁ	•—•	m	ㅌ	•—•	t
ㅂ	•—•	b/p	ㅍ	•—•	p
ㅅ	•—•	s/t	ㅍ	•—•	h/t

Ch 3 - 2

ㄱ ㄴ ㄷ ㄹ ㅁ ㅂ ㅅ

ㅇ ㅈ ㅊ ㅋ ㅌ ㅍ ㅎ

Ch 3-3

기	옥	에	이	옹	디	리	을	자	을	뜯	비
미	음	디	장	비	읃	미	옴	시	읏	합	읍
벽	조	긋	라	시	읏	르	틈	뷰	항	니	톱
니	피	읍	니	울	치	일	키	읔	옷	은	듬
흔	지	읒	온	옷	읓	리	읃	비	이	히	륙
이	옥	상	키	기	욕	울	곳	옵	응	옿	보
옹	인	피	수	랗	초	억	히	읗	질	잡	피
지	몇	읖	히	기	욕	보	티	달	공	리	읍
읒	른	튜	훟	찻	시	옷	읃	승	섭	를	디
치	기	역	키	봄	굽	니	치	면	나	후	저
춫	약	안	윽	욕	갿	윽	읒	놈	디	덩	컬
너	래	면	흘	티	읕	꼼	경	묵	귿	숲	견

Ch 3-4

ㄱ 기역 [gi-yeok]	ㄴ 니은 [ni-eun]	ㄷ 디귿 [di-geut]	ㄹ 리을 [ri-eul]
ㅁ 미음 [mi-eum]	ㅂ 비읍 [bi-eup]	ㅅ 시옷 [si-ot]	ㅇ 이응 [i-eung]
ㅈ 지읒 [ji-eut]	ㅊ 치읓 [chi-eut]	ㅋ 키읔 [ki-euk]	ㅌ 티읕 [ti-eut]
ㅍ 피읖 [pi-eup]	ㅎ 히읗 [hi-eut]		

Ch 3-5

a	ya	eo	yeo	o	yo	u	yu	eu	i
아	야	어	여	오	요	우	유	으	이

Ch 3-6

ム	ㅗ	ɷ	ㅈ	A	目	ひ	ᆜ	ㅏ	ㄹ
H	ㄱ	日	て	m	○	F	之	ㅍ	了
ろ	ヌ	子	ㅎ	中	ワ	ㄷ	日	F	ن
ㅍ	ㅑ	ㅂ	ㄴ	5	ㅅ	E	コ	ㅊ	V
月	ㅌ	ㅂ	ㅡ	ハ	Γ	Z	ㅋ	ㅛ	우

Ch 3-7

g	n	d	r	m	b	s
ㄱ	ㄴ	ㄷ	ㄹ	ㅁ	ㅂ	ㅅ

ng	j	ch	k	t	p	h
ㅇ	ㅈ	ㅊ	ㅋ	ㅌ	ㅍ	ㅎ

Ch 4-1

A. ⑤ [옫짱]
B. ④ [깍따]
C. ① [아거]
D. ② [꼳따발]
E. ③ [덥깨]
F. ④ [엽찝]
G. ③ [어리니]
H. ② [책쌍]
I. ③ [입꾸]
J. ② [미역꾹]

Ch 4-2

Butterfly [na-bi]		Sky [ha-neul]		Bicycle [ja-jeon-geo]			Cat [go-yang-i]		
나	비	하	늘	자	전	거	고	양	이
Today [o-neul]		**Now [ji-geum]**		**Puppy [gang-a-ji]**			**Cane [ji-pang-i]**		
오	늘	지	금	강	아	지	지	팡	이

A Answers

Ch 5 - 1

ㅐ	ae	Bad
ㅒ	yae	**Ya**m
ㅔ	e	Bed
ㅖ	ye	**Ye**s
ㅘ	wa	**Wa**ffle
ㅙ	wae	**Wa**gon
ㅚ	oe	**We**dding
ㅝ	wo	**Wo**nder
ㅞ	we	**We**dding
ㅟ	wi	**Wi**g
ㅢ	ui	**Eui**

Ch 5 - 2

ㅏ ㅐ ㅑ ㅒ ㅓ ㅔ ㅕ

ㅖ ㅗ ㅘ ㅙ ㅚ ㅛ ㅜ

ㅝ ㅞ ㅟ ㅠ ㅡ ㅢ ㅣ

Ch 5 - 3

ㅂ	夕	h	休	ㅞ	ㅜ	ㅑ	め	**ㅚ**	ㅘ
b	ㅞ	い	**ㅖ**	ㅛ	**ㅝ**	ル	ㅞ	夕	u
ㅙ	ケ	**ㅙ**	h	け	ㅘ	**ㅞ**	4	ㅠ	**ㅔ**
ㅏ	み	ㅟ	出	**ㅢ**	カ	[illegible]	は	夕	ㅣㅣ
川	ㅜ	**ㅟ**	ㅠ	セ	ㅓ	ㅝ	**ㅐ**	十	ん
ㅚ	千	八	ㅚ	ㅖ	り	二	五	ㅝ	ق

Ch - R

0. Tomato
1. Kiwi
2. France
3. Cola
4. Canada
5. Wine
6. Llama
7. Piano
8. Banana
9. Gorilla
10. Spain
11. Model
12. Coffee
13. Guitar
14. Brazil
15. Pickles
16. Puzzle
17. Pineapple
18. Mexico
19. Avocado
20. Cocktail
21. Wheelchair
22. Italy
23. Blueberries
24. Juice
25. Violin
26. Switzerland
27. Koala
28. Dress
29. Rhyme
30. Ketchup
32. Bus
33. Computer
34. Chimpanzee
34. Audio
35. Boxing
36. Sofa
37. Musicals
38. Panda
39. Royalty
40. Harp
41. Album
42. Shampoo
43. Know-how
44. Hamster
45. Donut
46. Pizza
47. Sauna
48. Hamburger
49. Interior
50. Kangaroos
51. Speaker
52. Hula Hoop
53. Massage
54. Tulip
55. Chocolate
56. System
57. Penguin
58. Design
59. Zigzag
60. Neon Sign
61. Goalkeeper
62. Bacteria
63. Chameleon

P 10 Days of Review : Romanized Pronunciations

R - D1 과일 [gwa-il]

귤 [gyul]
딸기 [ttal-gi]
복숭아[bokssung-a]
사과 [sa-gwa]
석류 [seongnyu]
수박 [su-bak]
용과 [yong-gwa]
자두 [ja-du]
자몽 [ja-mong]
포도 [po-do]

R - D2 채소 [chae-so]

가지 [ga-ji]
감자 [gam-ja]
당근 [dang-geun]
버섯 [beo-seot]
상추 [sang-chu]
양파 [yang-pa]
오이 [o-i]
옥수수 [ok-ssu-su]
피망 [pi-mang]
호박 [ho-bak]

R - D3 요일 [yo-il]

일주일 [il-jju-il]
요일 [yo-il]
월요일 [woryo-il]
화요일 [hwa-yo-il]
수요일 [su-yo-il]
목요일 [mogyo-il]
금요일 [geumyo-il]
토요일 [to-yo-il]
일요일 [iryo-il]
하루 [ha-ru]

R - D4 색깔 [saek-kkal]

빨강 [ppal-gang]
주황 [ju-hwang]
노랑 [no-rang]
초록 [cho-rok]
파랑 [pa-rang]
분홍 [bun-hong]
보라 [bo-ra]
하양 [ha-yang]
회색 [hoe-saek]
검정 [geom-jeong]

R - D5 국가[Guk-kka]

독일[do-gil]
멕시코[mek-ssi-ko]
미국[mi-guk]
영국[yeong-guk]
인도[in-do]
일본[il-bon]
중국[jung-guk]
캐나다[kae-na-da]
태국[tae-guk]
호주[ho-ju]

R - D6 대한민국 [dae-han-min-guk]

대한민국 [dae-han-min-guk]
한국 [han-guk]
태극기 [tae-geuk-kki]
한글 [han-geul]
한국어 [han-gu-geo]
한국인 [han-gu-gin]
한복 [han-bok]
남한-북한 [namhan-bukan]
조선 [jo-seon]
고려 [go-ryeo]

R - D7 모양 [mo-yang]

동그라미 [dong-geu-ra-mi]
세모 [se-mo]
삼각형 sam-ga-kyeong]
네모 [ne-mo]]
사각형 [sa-ga-kyeong]
마름모 [ma-reum-mo]
별모양 [byeol-mo-yang
반원 [ba-nwon]
타원 [ta-won]
원기둥 [won-gi-dung]

R - D8 탈 것

자동차 [ja-dong-cha]
기차 [gi-cha]
지하철 [ji-ha-cheol]
버스 [beo-seu]
자전거 [ja-jeon-geo]
배 [bae]
비행기 [bi-haeng-gi]
소방차 [so-bang-cha]
구급차 [gu-geup-cha]
경찰차 [gyeong-chal-cha]

R - D9,10 숫자 **[sut-jja]**

	Sino	Native
1	**일** [il]	**하나** [ha-na]
2	**이** [i]	**둘** [dul]
3	**삼** [sam]	**셋** [set]
4	**사** [sa]	**넷** [net]
5	**오** [o]	**다섯** [da-seot]
6	**육** [yuk]	**여섯** [yeo-seot]
7	**칠** [chil]	**일곱** [il-gop]
8	**팔** [pal]	**여덟** [yeo-deol]
9	**구** [gu]	**아홉** [a-hop]
10	**십** [sip]	**열** [yeol]

Made in the USA
Las Vegas, NV
18 August 2024